The Educator's Guide to Solutioning

The Educator's Guide to Solutioning

The Great Things That Happen When You Focus Students on Solutions, Not Problems

Willyn H. Webb

CORWIN PRESS, INC.
A Sage Publications Company
Thousand Oaks, California

For information address:

Corwin Press, Inc.
A Sage Publications Company
2455 Teller Road
Thousand Oaks, California 91320
E-mail: order@corwinpress.com

SAGE Publications Ltd.
6 Bonhill Street
London EC2A 4PU
United Kingdom

SAGE Publications India Pvt. Ltd.
M-32 Market
Greater Kailash I
New Delhi 110 048 India

Printed in the United States of America

Library of Congress Cataloging-in-Publication Data

Webb, Willyn H.
    The educator's guide to solutioning: The great things that
happen when you focus students on solutions, not problems /
Willyn H. Webb.
        p. cm.
    Includes bibliographical references and index.
    ISBN 0-8039-6748-9 (cloth: acid-free paper)
    ISBN 0-8039-6749-7 (pbk.: acid-free paper)
    1. Teacher-student relationships. 2. Effective teaching.
    3. Classroom management.   I. Title.
    LB1033.W37   1998
    371.102'3—ddc21   98-40073

This book is printed on acid-free paper.

99 00 01 02 03 04 10 9 8 7 6 5 4 3 2 1

Editorial Assistant: Julia Parnell
Production Editor: Wendy Westgate
Production Assistant: Stephanie Allen
Typesetter/Designer: Janelle LeMaster
Cover Designer: Tracy E. Miller

Contents

List of Reproducible Masters

Preface

*Solutioning is meant to enhance whatever
you are currently doing that works.*

**The Need for
Solutioning**

As educators, we are trained to *control* students' behavior, *tell* them how/what to learn, and *give* them the information they need to live successful lives. We are taught to see needs and to fill them. As an outcome, students are to become mature citizens, *acting* responsibly, *making* good decisions, and *finding* solutions to the world's problems. What a mixed message! It is time to remedy this contradiction by adopting a solutioning focus and using the language of solutioning for problem-solving, management, and dignified interactions. This book will empower readers to be solutioning-focused educators. By viewing student behavior and performance differently, by asking instead of telling, and by seeing competencies instead of deficits, educators can empower students with the responsibility and ability to meet the needs of the society they will be facing as adults.

Each year, we as educators are to cover more—not only the content but also responsibility, self-esteem, reasoning, problem solving, and critical thinking, to name a few. Imagine if all of the above could be available for students by altering just slightly the *way* we teach and interact with students instead of increasing the *what. Solutioning* is more than a problem-solving technique, a conflict mediation program, discipline, classroom management, self-esteem, critical thinking, positive assessment, or empowerment; it is a focus backed up with the language to make all of these happen. Solutioning is not meant to replace, but to enhance, whatever you are currently doing that works. Why not save time, teach responsibility, and find solutions by blending in the solutioning process with a few new questions?

Through my workshops and classes, I have found that all educators (classroom teachers, administrators) at all levels want to be positive with students but that many need the language tools to make it happen. Some have had the discipline techniques they were trained in and successful with taken away and are looking to replace those with more solution-oriented interventions. Others are doing an excellent job and want even more ways to maintain their positive focus in these demanding times. All teachers want to manage their classrooms positively, empower students to be responsible, set up students to earn self-esteem, and leave feeling inspired rather than burned out. Solutioning meets these needs and the needs of all educators looking to be the best they can be.

The Birth of Solutioning

Discipline becomes a non-issue, even in middle school.

I came to teaching with what I now call "the solutioning focus." I saw children as human beings and wanted to give them the responsibility and respect of human beings. I was not interested in controlling, telling, and forcing my students in any way. The language and techniques both to implement this philosophy and to have a well-disciplined learning environment at the same time were something I did not have. During my master's degree program in counseling, I was exposed to language from solution-focused brief therapy that enhanced my classroom management more than any discipline classes. Working together, taking individual responsibility, choices, exceptions, and solutioning (later) focused communication made my classroom thrive, and discipline became a non-issue, even in middle school. I never "counseled" classroom students; I just worked with them, rather than try to control them. I would question and allow them to come up with solutions, rather than tell them what to do. I would end each day, not tired or burned out, but energized and ready for the next.

The first solution-focused question I adopted was, How do you want things to be? The first time I used it, it just popped out. I had Robert in the hall for disciplinary action. It was the policy of the school to take students aside and *tell* them in a firm manner exactly what was expected. As a beginning middle school teacher, discipline and control were crucial for establishing an environment conducive to learning. I was told I needed to establish a "strict" reputation in order to have controlled classes.

What a Surprise!

Robert and I looked at each other, both dreading what was to come. When I opened my mouth, I did not *recite* the rules (he knew them), but *asked* Robert, "How do you want things to be?" His response was not what I had expected. I now think of it as a meltdown. This frustrating young man had feelings, desires, and abilities. He shared some great possibilities for improvement, and I followed through with, "What can *you* do *instead* to make it that way?" Together, we explored what was different when things were better and cocreated a **plan** we felt good about and could make happen under the school's expectations for us both!

The greatest outcome was during that moment we joined forces and set out against problem behaviors so that 2nd-hour English class would be successful, which it eventually was, for both of us. Solutioning was the recipe I needed to create students who controlled their own choices and behaviors. I loved not having to do it for them. With that burden lifted, the discipline and learning followed. Talk about killing two birds with one stone! By empowering students, encouraging their input, and cocreating solutions, I became a happier, better teacher who had partnerships with students. After all, I was not only interacting in a positive, forward-moving manner but also incorporating a life skill for dealing with problems and finding solutions—the ultimate life skill that results in what is most demanded by society: capable, responsible individuals.

Solution-focused language, strategies, and thinking were originally developed in the mental health field and have since been used successfully in a variety of settings: *therapy* (Andrews & Andrews, 1995; Budman & Gurman, 1988; de Shazer, 1988; de Shazer et al., 1986; Dolan, 1991; Friedman & Fanger, 1991; Furman & Ahola, 1992; Huber & Backlund, 1996; Juhnke & Coker, 1997; Juhnke & Osborne, 1997; Molnar & de Shazer, 1987; O'Hanlon & Weiner-Davis, 1989; Walter & Peller, 1992); *pediatrics* (Klar & Colman, 1995); *nursing* (Mason, Breen, & Whipple 1994; Tuyn, 1992); *employee assistance programs* (Czyzewski, 1996); *adventure experiences* (Gass & Gillis, 1995); *parenting* (Metcalf, 1997); *home preservation programs* (Washburn, 1994); and *school counseling* (Bonnington, 1993; Downing & Harrison, 1992; Kral & Kowalski, 1989; Metcalf, 1995; Murphy, 1994; Rhodes, 1993) under the solution-focused label, among others. Although now used in therapy as well (Webb, 1998), solutioning was developed for education. In this book, I am not adapting a useful technique from other areas; rather, I am sharing my successful use of solutioning (and those of my adult students and workshop participants) from the classroom.

Anyone who interacts with students can benefit from the life-changing focus and simple language techniques of solutioning.

The Simple Power of Solutioning

After the first weekend of my solutioning course, the participants leave in agreement over the need but a little overwhelmed with all the new language. The role plays seem unnatural, and the participants are nervous about trying the questions on their two case study students. After doing so and experiencing the power of the language, however, they come back the second weekend with a little sparkle in their eyes. They like students' reactions and are anxious to practice more, learn more, and head back to the front lines. Two weeks later, during the final weekend of the course, they come back sold hook, line, and sinker on solutioning. Their case study presentations are celebrations of success! They want to share the ideas in their schools, and many have had me come to their schools to do workshops. Consistently, these adult students share that changing the focus of their interactions and environment from problems and deficits, from telling and controlling, to successes, exceptions, skills, and competencies through asking, interacting, cocreating, and working with students against problems has refreshed them and enriched their students. Their case studies provided me with enough motivation to write this book and make solutioning available for all educators. Anyone who interacts with students can benefit from the life-changing focus and simple language techniques of solutioning.

For example, when a student makes an achievement, instead of your responding with a compliment like, "Good job," give the student authority by adding, "How did you do that?"

Josh

Josh was not what you would call a highly successful student. He struggled with the assignments but tried hard. One day, he was the first student to complete a short quiz. When he brought it up to hand it in, I commented, "Wow, Josh, you're the first one done. How did you do that?" (I knew he had studied hard.) He looked puzzled and then beamed with the knowledge that he had learned the material. Watching his face as he processed my question in his head was awesome. During that moment, *he figured out for himself that he was capable.* I doubt that this process would have happened with a simple, "Way to go."

I found most reactions equally interesting and valuable. Students were obviously not in the habit of realizing for themselves their own skills or acknowledging exceptions to problems. With simple questions like, "How did you do that?" students will truly know and own their abilities, talents, problem exceptions, and reasons for successes and use them to take responsibility and solve problems.

The Educator's Guide to Solutioning

Through questions, the power is taken away from the problem.

Becoming adept at solutioning does not require you to start from the beginning of this book and continue through to the end, completing every task and trying every suggestion. Instead, you may integrate one part at a time by beginning with what feels good or seems to match your teaching and interacting style. The results will be so motivating that the rest will follow. Treat this guide as a smorgasbord of ideas. Sample as the appetite allows. When you're full, stop. When the next problem student whets the appetite again, open it back up and try a new solutioning technique. Solutioning is not designed to replace anything or to require radical changes, but to build upon and accentuate the great things you, your students, and their parents are already doing.

Chapter 1 introduces the solutioning focus and illustrates the importance of the language. It sets you on your way to realizing and using your own solution capabilities while overviewing the 3-P solutioning process, which can be used as a whole or in parts, randomly or in a planned interaction/conference.

Chapter 2 starts the journey through the solutioning map with the **purpose,** where teacher and student become partners against problems. Through questions, the power is taken away from the problem, and the talk shifts toward a more positive **purpose.** The tools of externalizing, labelizing, normalizing, and temporizing allow teachers to assist students in establishing a joint **purpose.** When students are no longer considered to be or feel like *the* problem, burdens are lifted and solutions emerge. Results of maintaining or solving are considered, and students are motivated toward action. Sometimes just a new view of the problem and more purposeful thinking begin positive change.

Chapter 3 takes you on to the **potentials,** the heart of solutioning, where exceptions to problem and possible solutions are illuminated. Through questioning, students are empowered to find/construct solutions from within. Solutioning provides four areas of exploration: *past* and *present,* where exceptions to problems give clues to solutions; *pretend,* where visualizations provide behaviors to try; and *people,* from whom successful solutions are borrowed. Students usually discover their own solutions after only a few questions. "When isn't the problem happening, and what is different then?" is a common **potentials** question.

Chapter 4 discusses the **plan,** which is based on the **potentials** just shared. Empower students to choose the **plan** that is right for their level of readiness: positive, practice, or perform. A *positive plan* to notice what works or to discover when things are better will enable students to shift their focus away from problems and toward solutions. A *practice plan* encourages doing nothing yet while visualizing a rehearsal of the solution, which in most cases actually happens. A *perform plan* meets the "Fab Five" criteria: specifically stating what the student will do (e.g., not others or what he or she will not, an end state, a wish), beginning immediately.

Chapter 5 encourages **progress**—following up and ensuring that solutions last. Taking the initial success and helping students realize it, own it, and continue to use it is the cement of solutioning and the hallmark of responsibility and self-esteem. The techniques in this chapter can be used with any achievement, improvement, or growth in all aspects of learning and interacting.

Chapter 6 encourages "Why stop now?" by illustrating solutioning's applicability to discipline, classroom management, lesson planning, assessing, critical thinking, decision making, and lifelong learning.

Chapter 7 takes solutioning into conflict mediation, parent-teacher communications/conferences, staffings, and meetings.

Reproducible MASTERS to accompany each chapter contain Language Lessons, practice scenarios, conversation helpsheets, student worksheets, and many immediately usable ideas. Comparison charts are used throughout the chapters to illustrate the differences between a problem focus and the solutioning focus. These are not black-and-white representations. Many areas are gray, and many overlap. Approach them generally, noticing the power of solutioning in making a positive difference. Fictitious names are used in the examples and case studies, which are not designed to provide a perfect way of handling a situation, but rather illustrate the use of solutioning. To be truly effective, every interaction with students should unfold sincerely and uniquely.

If you are ready to approach your students with a positive, forward-moving focus, ready to use new language that accentuates competencies, and ready to be more efficient and less stressed, then read on. No matter how you choose to use this book—adopting a few powerful questions or using the entire 3-P process—remember that students are capable; they do have abilities, feelings, past experiences, and future desires, all of which influence strongly what they do and the success level they can reach; and *they* are the future.

—Willyn H. Webb

Acknowledgments

Without the inspiration, encouragement, and support of the adult students who have taken my solutioning courses and workshops, a book would never have entered my mind. Without the birth, love, and patience of my daughter, Skylyn, I would not have had the courage and faith to leave full-time education, and the doorway of authorship would not have been opened.

Without the praise, support, and nudging of Alice Foster at Corwin Press, the pursuit of writing this book would have ended prematurely. Without the time, love, and support of my family and my husband, I would not have been able to persist in the demands of authorship. Without the Delta, Colorado, library staff and Mary Mills, I would not have had resources or proper grammar. Without Kelli Hepler (educator characters) and Dana Wolf (student characters), I would not have had illustrations. Without the positive interactions I experienced with students of all ages during the evolution of solutioning and the refinement of the language, it would not be at all. Thank you everyone.

It seems unfair to summarize so quickly the major contributions of the above-named individuals. Behind it all, however, solutioning has come from God. I have known this from the beginning, and solutioning would not have developed without Him. Harry Allen, in *Decision* (1998), expresses my acknowledgement for *The Educator's Guide to Solutioning*: "As God has seen fit to use me, anything I have achieved has been through God's grace. To God be all the glory."

About the Author

Willyn H. Webb, M.A., L.P.C., N.C.C., is dedicated to empowering the solutioning focus. An enthusiastic educator, she has experience teaching all grade levels, from kindergarten to adult, and is currently an Adjunct Professor for Adams State College, Alamosa, Colorado. A licensed and nationally certified therapist, she is in part-time private practice solutioning with children and adolescents, their families, and their schools. Honored in *Who's Who Among American Teachers,* she is the author of *Solutioning: Solution-Focused Interventions for Counselors.*

A motivating presenter, Willyn has conducted workshops for the Colorado Association of Middle Level Educators, the School Counselors Association, and at the Colorado Effective Education Model Conference, among others. In-service workshops and classes for school districts, spreading the language and focus of solutioning, are her favorites. For further information on Willyn Webb's workshops, contact her at Solutioning Counseling and Consulting, 117 Meeker Street #7, Delta, CO 81416; phone (970) 250-6306; fax (970) 874-8002; e-mail: cwebbd@aol.com.

An energized individual, Willyn is the mother of Skylyn (age 3) and Joyclie (age 3 weeks), rancher, and Boston marathon qualifier. With her Christian faith and the shared experiences of her trainees as primary motivators, she wants all students to experience the empowerment, dignity, pride, ability, and responsibility of interacting with educators who have the solutioning focus and speak the language of solutioning.

This book is dedicated to Skylyn,
who made the supreme sacrifice of
sharing her mommy with it.

1

Pack Your Bags

*More learning, growth, responsibility, and work than
ever before will happen as a result of solutioning.*

Imagine for a moment your last vacation. Feel the feelings, see the sights, and relive the moments. Relaxed and fun, or hectic and troublesome? Most people enjoy a vacation even though it may contain more stress than staying home and in the routine. Perhaps this is because the emphasis is on what went right—the fun parts, the attractions, the interactions—rather than on the inconveniences, the crowds, or the hassles. This phenomenon has been referred to by some as the *vacation mind-set*. It may be an attitude, a positive outlook, a determination to enjoy; most of all, it is a focus. Focusing on what works!

Could such a focus be put into place in your life? In your classroom? In your students' minds? Is there a way to begin seeing the exceptions to the rules, the successes amid the failures, the growth despite the problems? Yes. Solutioning will create a vacation mind-set for your classroom. Don't let the word *vacation* and its connotation of no work, relaxation, and all fun mislead you. More learning, growth, responsibility, and work than ever before will happen as a result of solutioning.

This chapter illustrates the solutioning focus, what it is and what it isn't, and prepares you for a journey through solutioning, learning the 3-P process that empowers the actualization of the focus. The luggage needed for solutioning is the focus, the language, and you, what you are already doing that works. Examine each of these as you pack.

*By practicing a solutioning focus, you will get what
you want, look for, and believe about students.*

Suitcase 1: Focus

We are not born seeing the glass half empty or half full, being controlled by life or controlling it, enjoying it or surviving it. Each day is filled with small but very significant choices about what we focus on, the language we use, the messages we give, and the route our interactions take. "We go toward what we focus on" (Vannoy, 1994, p. 41). What choices have you been making? What are you going toward and focusing on?

MASTER 1 "Focus Self-Test" will give you an idea of where you are now and where you will be going with solutioning. *Quickly* answer the questions. Tabulate your score and read the interpretations. Are you acting out the focus you want or claim to have? How close are you to a solutioning focus? What kind of difference will the solutioning focus make in your classroom?

MASTER 1
Focus Self-Test

1. What do you focus on at school?
   a. Skills, abilities, what works
   b. Needs to fill, problems to fix, students to control
   c. Just coping: lesson plans due, grades need figuring, duty tonight
2. What messages do you say to yourself regarding lessons?
   a. Get through it, get it covered so that we keep up with the other teacher
   b. Enjoy it: an opportunity to be creative, enjoy learning with students
   c. An obstacle: boring to most students, too difficult for many, impossible to individualize or make fun
3. How do you see your students?
   a. Hassles
   b. Joys
   c. A group you see every day that gives you headaches most of the time
4. How do you see students' potentials?
   a. Frustrating
   b. Capable
   c. Some of both
5. What are your interactions with students like?
   a. Conversations
   b. Wars
   c. Instructing
6. How do you feel?
   a. Stuck
   b. Barely keeping your head above water
   c. Forward moving
7. Who controls your classroom?
   a. You as supreme authority
   b. The students because there is no discipline and they are not responsible
   c. There is no need for control; you work together
8. Who is the expert?
   a. The students because they think they know everything and won't listen
   b. You because you have a college degree
   c. Everyone has various areas of expertise that can be used
9. Which of these questions can you answer most quickly?
   a. What are the problems in your classroom?
   b. What works in your classroom?
   c. Who is to blame for the problems in your classroom?
10. Which of these questions can you answer most quickly?
    a. Which students are troublesome in your school/classroom?
    b. What abilities, exceptions, and potentials do those students have?
    c. What are the reasons these students are troublesome?

(continued)

MASTER 1 Continued

11. Where is your attention?
    a. Curriculum, grading
    b. Discipline, control
    c. Interactions, solutions
12. Which of these do you think is most important for students to gain from their education?
    a. Content
    b. Study skills
    c. Responsibility, decision making, self-control

Think about: Are you cultivating habits that are helpful to your defined purpose for entering education?

Is what you say that you want your teaching to stand for consistent with what it really illustrates?

What is your focus, and how is it reflected in your view of yourself, your language, and your interactions with students?

Scoring:

1. Give yourself 3 for a, 1 for b, 2 for c.
2. Give yourself 2 for a, 3 for b, 1 for c.
3. Give yourself 1 for a, 3 for b, 2 for c.
4. Give yourself 1 for a, 3 for b, 2 for c.
5. Give yourself 3 for a, 1 for b, 2 for c.
6. Give yourself 2 for a, 1 for b, 3 for c.
7. Give yourself 2 for a, 1 for b, 3 for c.
8. Give yourself 1 for a, 2 for b, 3 for c.
9. Give yourself 2 for a, 3 for b, 1 for c.
10. Give yourself 1 for a, 3 for b, 2 for c.
11. Give yourself 2 for a, 1 for b, 3 for c.
12. Give yourself 1 for a, 2 for b, 3 for c.

If you scored 36-26: You have a positive, solutioning focus! Your classroom must be an enjoyable place to be. By already seeing the potentials, the solutions, and the exceptions, you will quickly adapt the language of solutioning and get your students on the same, solutioning-focused page. If it works, do more of it, with solutioning!

If you scored 25-15: You have great intentions and are already encouraging positive interactions. With a little solutioning language and practice, both you and your students will enjoy living and experiencing a solutioning focus. The differences will happen quickly and naturally for you with just a few new questions or phrases from solutioning!

If you scored 14 and under: Seems like you have a tough situation and are doing a great job coping. But, "if it doesn't work, do something different!" (Carpenter, 1997, p. 117). With the language of solutioning, both you and your students will begin seeing and creating exceptions to the problems and frustrations—building onto and experiencing a solutioning focus where things do work.

Chart 1.1　The Focus

Problem-Focused	*Solutioning-Focused*
Excuses	Exceptions
Fixing	Creating
Stuck	Forward moving
Deficits and needs	Abilities and resources
Failures	Successes
Blaming	Partnering
What is NOT working	What IS working
Past	Present and future
What's wrong?	What's right?
Problem	Purpose
Control	Responsibility

Now that you are aware of your own outlook, consider the solutioning focus by looking at the Chart 1.1. What exactly does this focus include? Disclude? The chart is not black or white, as we all are "on the fence" at times. This results in many mixed messages (for both our students and ourselves). Do you consider yourself forward moving but waste time searching for causes of problems? Do you say you see the good in students but then find yourself pointing out their mistakes (even with the good intentions of correction)? Do you believe in students' abilities but find yourself trying to fix their problems? Do you subscribe to responsibility-giving, student-centered methods but begin telling and controlling at the first sign of a problem? Do you consider yourself a problem solver but have a list of excuses for every less-than-perfect aspect of your classroom? Are you or your students playing the blame game even though you are working toward how you want things to be? Are exceptional or problem-free times discussed during conferences or meetings that are supposedly positive?

> *By practicing a solutioning focus, you will get what*
> *you want, look for, and believe about students.*

Students will see their abilities, the exceptions to their problems, solutions they can create, and decisions they can make while taking responsibility. What curriculum could be more powerful or life affecting? So, how do you get it, do it, share it with students? Start by avoiding mixed messages and an inconsistent focus while creating the solutioning focus by not worrying about causes, forgetting blaming altogether, and always remembering hope. Let's pack your solutioning focus bag.

The Cause: An Unnecessary Item

Don't you just love to go to the teachers' workroom and listen? Few places are more filled with excuses.

"No wonder Lisa is failing math; her dad is an alcoholic."

"Ever since Tim's parents got divorced, he hasn't put out any effort."

"If the special ed teacher would quit babying him, he might get in gear."

"I don't understand why Roberto won't try in my class. He seems smart."

"There is no way he can pass third grade with that attitude."

"She'll go to high school and get pregnant; that's what her sisters did."

"If they had learned their math facts in elementary school, I wouldn't be having all these problems now. What are those teachers doing?"

"She's in a gang; look at her clothes."

"These kids come into high school without knowing any grammar. I think they must just play at the middle school."

"Most students from single-parent homes have behavior problems."

Sound familiar? Through many of these excuses, educators are sincerely attempting to find out why students are not having success. The whys do not automatically provide solutions and often point to areas where educators rarely have any impact or control. How many times have you heard that the school cannot really do anything to help the student because "You can't change the family" or that students can't be motivated to learn because the parents don't have (or value) an education or because the home life is just too challenging, and on and on? Some teachers use this as a license to give up on certain students or to justify failure. Others are sincerely attempting to help students, believing that a cause is the first step. Our culture seems to be hooked on a need to understand a problem before attempting to solve it, thus wasting time and building excuses, never getting around to solutions. Causes rarely facilitate positive change.

Instead, look for times when students were having success or were doing better, find out what they were doing then, and have them try to do some of or more of that now. *Instead,* explore with students how they want things (that they can control) to be and the behaviors that may begin to get them there. *Instead,* help students consider how others may handle their situation and find some success so that they may try out those behaviors. In other words, get out of the past and into the future, out of the causes and into trying possible solutions or parts of possible solutions. The talk is about how things can be, not about how bad or why they are now.

What About Bob?
A first experience with solutioning

(Used by permission from Dottie Miller)

Bob was a fourth-grade pupil of Dottie Miller, a student in my solutioning-focused interventions class. Bob had come to Dottie with a poor recommendation. His previous teachers had concluded that support at home was worse than none, that he had ADD, was unmotivated, and would never succeed. They thought he was just one of those with whom they had to deal until he dropped out. He was the one of whom teachers say you're doing the best you can if you keep him from inhibiting the learning of others. Dottie, however, did not subscribe to this way of thinking. She was not going to give up on Bob and baby-sit him. She wanted to teach him, help him overcome his obstacles, and have him find some success in school. Dottie chose Bob for her case study in my class.

The first night, she described Bob as having "meltdowns" from which he could not recover for the rest of the day. Most directions or corrections from the teacher or other students could cause meltdowns. The meltdowns included crying, yelling, and out-of-control behavior. Dottie related some of the background information described earlier. We decided right then that none of the strikes against Bob would be the focus. Her **purpose** (as was Bob's) was to overcome the meltdowns. A behavioral program was already in place with daily checks and a weekly reward of a trip to the computer room.

The first change Dottie made was to begin noticing when Bob was not melting down. She would then point this out to Bob and follow up with an exception question—for example, "Bob, you've been in your seat listening for the past 10 minutes. How did you do that?" To Dottie's surprise, in a short time Bob not only increased the amount of time he could go without melting down but also could give her behaviorally stated reasons why—for example, "I just didn't look at the other kids when they teased me," or, "I just told myself I could keep from crying at least until recess, and I did it."

Dottie then arranged a time to speak alone with Bob. Their conversation began like this:

Dottie: Bob, I'm so impressed with how you have been controlling your behavior lately. Let's talk about how you've been doing it and about a **plan** we could come up with to continue this trend.

Bob gave her all of the answers, and the meltdowns eventually subsided to the point that other concerns could be solutioned as well. Because Dottie did not concern herself with all of the reasons *why* Bob struggled, but rather looked at the times when his behavior was acceptable and helped him see his abilities, she enabled Bob to succeed.

Forget Blaming

Make the problem something the student can overcome.

Not only do educators find themselves blaming, but students are also products of a society that plays what Susan Stewart (1996) calls "the blame game." "Victimhood is definitely in. Kids seem to be born with a blaming instinct" (p. 3). Why not? If someone can get $3 million for spilling hot coffee, why not point out your reasons for not doing your homework? The "blame" may be just as valid. Often, the problem's control over the student comes from its power as an excuse (Bob had everyone convinced). Solutioning uses externalizing (Chapter 2) to give the responsibility and the control to the student by making the problem something the student can overcome.

Even valid blame and excuses, which do exist, can become less powerful when the problem is externalized. Some students are doing the best they can in their situations. They need to be commended and supported. One way to support is to help them not fall victim to the blame game. We have all had the student for whose life circumstances we truly have compassion. Yet, we feel "taken" as the student uses the situation for all it's worth. Taking away their crutch is the only way these students will learn to walk. It is so easy to buy in to their sad stories, but in doing this we move them from the crutch to the wheelchair. Solutioning uses reflection and a purpose to empower, as opposed to the sympathy and "fixing" of many traditional methods, which tend to make teachers the experts, further depowering students.

Solutioning takes away from both student and educator the need for blaming; it does this by finding ways to make things how both want them to be, perhaps by using what has been better or more hopeful before! One solution is always obvious for a student who has many excuses and many people to blame: "You've gotten this far despite those circumstances. You really can cope. How did you deal with everything and get to school today . . . ?" Giving students the message that the problems in their lives are not problems with them, just inconveniences or intrusions that are temporary and solvable, is very empowering, refreshing, and motivating.

Always Remember Hope

Being solutioning focused is seeing students, families, and all other individuals as having the abilities and resources necessary to flourish, grow, develop, and solve problems. Solutioning is not giving directions, telling, disciplining, or problem solving. Solutioning is getting from students definitions of a purpose, their past successes or current exceptions, and their solutions. The solutioning focus assumes exceptions to problems (or times when they are not as intense). Negative behavior, low skills, or problems cannot happen 100% of the time (Metcalf, 1995). No behavior happens all the time (even Bob's meltdowns). Thus, the solutioning focus builds hope, helps students see the exceptions, and sets them up to find solutions.

A hopeful view of change contributes to a solutioning-focused, growth-oriented, and proactive environment where few interventions to problems are needed. It is times when students are not succeeding or following our rules and procedures that we most think of and desire to change. Change is behind discipline, punishment, and rewards. Not unlike any of the above, solutioning provides ways to create change. Viewing students as always changing prevents labeling, and interactions happen where exceptions are always being examined, leading directly to positive change (Webb, 1999).

Clowning Around

Sent in by a solutioning workshop participant

Reuben was the class clown, a kid everyone liked. Despite Reuben's talent with humor and a quick mind, he lacked the motivation to turn in his assignments. Conferences were held, and the parents shared all of the numerous attempts they had used to get Reuben in gear. They thought Reuben was intelligent but had gotten behind, and they were frustrated with his lack of effort. As his teacher, I shared with them all of the attempts I had made to help motivate Reuben as well. The empathy of the conference was nice, but solutions were not developed and Reuben probably felt blamed. This was before solutioning.

During the solutioning workshop, Reuben and his parents immediately came to mind. I went back to school and arranged another conference. With the belief that change is constant, this conference emphasized how even though Reuben seemed stuck, he was changing. I used solutioning questioning, and Reuben began to see how he was changing to avoid the work and would continue having to change: more jokes, more antics, more trouble. With questions like, "When aren't you clowning, and what is different then?" and "What would it be like if you found a solution and were not in trouble so much?" the focus of the conference went from past to future, from us controlling Reuben, attempting to understand why, trying to manipulate his behavior, and setting up systems of bribery, to him taking responsibility for his behavior. When he was questioned and his opinion sought, he saw that we were teaming up against the problem (clowning) together, changing together, with him as our guide. Reuben did begin to guide, sharing how he put all of his efforts into ways of not doing the work, rather than attempting to do it and possibly failing. In his mind (as in the minds of many others), it was much better to fail for not doing the work than to do failing work. In fact, he said he was getting tired of figuring out ways to avoid assignments and of the consequences. He was uneasy, however, about what the other students would think if he changed and was no longer the class clown.

Through **potentials** questions like "What is effective for avoiding the work, and how could that be used?" we discussed his abilities rather than his deficits (like before). This showed some great creative skills, some organizational skills, and many public speaking and communication skills, skills Reuben was very happy to learn he had. His self-confidence began to improve, which was very motivating for him. To make a long story short, Reuben gained the confidence to try some of his (preexisting) skills on his assignments and experienced some small successes (problem exceptions) on which to build. He could do this without becoming a "nerd" because he was using the same abilities he had in being the class clown. He was not changing who he was, just how he chose to use his abilities.

Acknowledging constant change enlightens exceptions that are bound to have happened sometime or are happening a little bit now. Realizing the inevitable quality of change puts us in a position to begin helping students make their desired movie, videotaping each day as it comes. The relationship is enhanced, and the interactions become productive.

Starting a small change may be as simple as "asking a student to do something different the next time something doesn't work" (Metcalf, 1995, p. 22). In fact, a small change in one part of a student's life often creates a ripple effect in other areas (O'Hanlon & Weiner-Davis, 1989). By getting the ball rolling with a small success/exception, students are in a better position or state of mind to find solutions to other, more difficult problems (Webb, 1999). The solutioning focus uses minute positives and fleeting exceptions in breaking problems and building solutions. The following case study illustrates a rapid ripple effect of change as provided by one of my educator students.

Jake, the Fit Fighter

Contributed by Lyndall Hamilton, kindergarten aide (Used by permission from Lyndall Hamilton)

Jake had fits at least three times a week, usually sometime in the morning. One morning after learning some solutioning language, I simply asked Jake, "Would you like to fight off the 'fits' (his description) just for today?" (externalize problem) Jake looked confused at first but then answered that he wasn't sure whether he could. I replied, "It's 9:45, and you have not had a fit yet this morning. (exception) How have you done that?"

Jake replied, "I just did it!" I reminded Jake when he continued to fight off the fits and asked him, "How are you doing this?" Jake did not have a fit that day and decreased his fits to once every 2 or 3 weeks. He got to go out to recess almost all the time. As I learned about notes and certificates at the end of the solutioning class, I decided to make one for Jake. It was an award for a champion Fit Fighter. Jake beamed with pride when I gave it to him. Before solutioning, I had mainly noticed and interacted with Jake when he was having a fit or about to have a fit by trying to control it or stop it. When I changed my focus to the non-fit times, even 45 minutes of small change, the rest just followed. It was so easy! What a subtle but powerful difference the focus and language of solutioning make.

By changing how this kindergarten student viewed his ability to control his emotions, the ripple effect began and the problem was on its way out. The ideas students have about their problems encourage or discourage the likelihood of solutions. Controlling outbursts is more doable than stopping them altogether.

Whether or not you have hope comes out in the messages and meanings behind your words, and it all builds from there. On which side of Chart 1.1 are you putting yourself? What kinds of relationships do you have with students? Traveling through the remainder of this book, adopting a solution-

Chart 1.2   Focused Interactions

Problem-Focused	Solutioning-Focused
Telling and controlling	Asking and involving
Cut down	Build up
Enforcement	Interaction
Overlook small change	Build on small change
Frustrating	Exciting
Blaming	Partnering
Teacher as authority/expert	Teacher as leader
Wallowing in the mud	Envisioning a desired tomorrow
Blaming parents	Teaming up with parents
Opposition	Trust
Teacher input only	Student input valued
Reactions	Relationships
Critical	Encouraging

ing focus, and implementing it with students will take you from the problem side to the solutioning side. Look at the difference in the quality of interactions in Chart 1.2.

Ready for a solutioning focus?

When you pause as the final bell rings, what is usually on your mind—the problems of the day, the hassles, or everything you need to do to be ready for tomorrow?

When you walk through the door at home and someone asks how your day was, do you usually start with the good events or the bad?

If you are like the majority, you unload all the horrors and then get caught up in doing things that need to be done at home before ever getting to the good. Generally, we focus on problems (sometimes trying to outdo each other), rather than the opposite, times when life is working. In fact, a word for the opposite of problems is somewhat lacking. What does it say about our focus that a word fitting this description is missing from our vocabulary? Solution may be the opposite of problem, but what about the times that are not problematic, yet are not a solution to something either—they are just working. It is these times that we may have forgotten. (Webb, 1999, pp. 26-27)

These are the times that solutioning empowers students, teachers, and parents to shift their focus and to do more. The solutioning educator sees exceptions where others see problems, potentials where others see complaints and failures.

Chart 1.3   Language

Problem-Focused	Solutioning-Focused
"Sit down and get to work."	"What is happening during the times when you are learning? What are you doing then?"
"It's for your own good."	"How do you want things to be?"
"Because it's the rule."	"What will happen as a result of maintaining or solving?"
"Don't talk."	"How do you control talking?"
"You've got the ability; if only you'd do your work."	"What is different about the times when you do your work?"
"You need to get in gear if you want to pass."	"When you are passing, what will you be doing differently?"
"You'll spend the year in the principal's office."	"Pretend you are acting respectfully and tell it to me like a movie."
Labels	Normalized descriptions
Monologue	Dialogue
Statements	Questions

Suitcase 2: Language

Through language, we portray our focus, use our strengths, and empower students toward solutions.

Language is what you experience as you journey through the solutioning process of this book. Through careful attention to our words, we can channel students' thinking away from negative labels or distinctions and toward solutions. By shifting interactions from problem talk, which closes all possibilities for change, to solution talk, which assumes that positive change will happen, you can alter the view and begin the change process. As a quick example, to a student who says, "I will never pass math," the math teacher might respond, "So far, you haven't passed math." This response puts the problem in the past and encourages the possibility of a different future. Very few choices that we make each day affect our students, their views, their learning, and our interactions with them as powerfully as our words (see Chart 1.3 and MASTER 2 "Reflection: What Would You Say").

Notice the difference between what happens when one says to him/herself, "I have failed three times" and what happens when he/she says, "I am a failure." (S. I. Hayakawa *[sic]* in *Webster's*, 1992, p. 92)

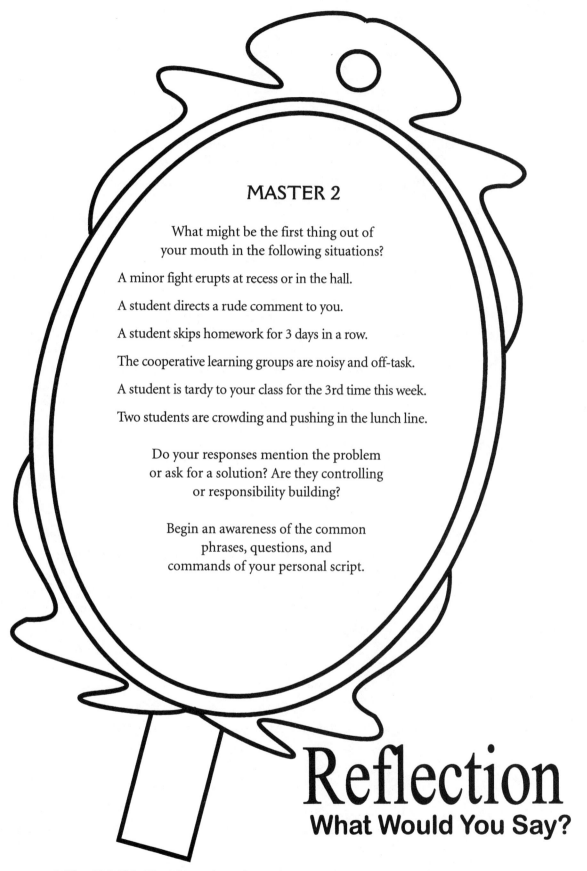

MASTER 2

What might be the first thing out of
your mouth in the following situations?

A minor fight erupts at recess or in the hall.

A student directs a rude comment to you.

A student skips homework for 3 days in a row.

The cooperative learning groups are noisy and off-task.

A student is tardy to your class for the 3rd time this week.

Two students are crowding and pushing in the lunch line.

Do your responses mention the problem
or ask for a solution? Are they controlling
or responsibility building?

Begin an awareness of the common
phrases, questions, and
commands of your personal script.

Reflection
What Would You Say?

You all know where you want to be and what you want from students, but you may not have a personal script that gets you there. Perhaps you think you will be abdicating your authority by sharing responsibility for solutions with students. Solutioning is not about talking the talk, it is about walking the walk through talk. Many questions teachers are in the habit of asking are the regurgitation of information or the "guess what's in my head" type. These are appropriate at times, but not during solutioning. How are students going to learn to think if they are not asked for input and then not respected for it when it comes?

Solutioning questions are open ended, not the yes-or-no type. Asking a few of the right questions will lead you in the direction you want to go with students. These questions value and respect students' individual thoughts, exceptions, potentials, and ideas. The 3-P process is designed not only to encourage students' input but also to use the input to build solutions. For the first time, a process exists that truly respects student ideas, thus building responsibility, self-esteem, and solutions that will really happen and really work.

Solutioning is more than problem solving. It brings creativity, integrity, and respect to every interaction you have with students. By placing extreme importance on each word that comes out of your mouth, especially those common questions and phrases that seem to be part of your personal script, you make each conversation a learning experience. Whether it is testable learning or not, in time it will be the most beneficial. As you read through the Language Lessons in the following chapters, star the questions/phrases you like the best, try them first, and after the initial inspiring results, come back for more. You may want to copy the Language Lessons and use them as "cheat sheets" during conversations and conferences. A word of caution: If you try them all at once, you may be overwhelmed. One question can make a difference.

Suitcase 3: You   *The solutions, the answers, and the abilities are within you,*
within your students, and within their parents.

Seeing yourself as talented, capable, exceptional, and ready to implement solutioning is the final item needed for this journey. Begin practicing the solutioning focus by answering the following questions:

What's working for me?

How do I want things to be?

What is the best thing that has happened this day, week, year?

What have I done well in the past that I could do again?

What are my students and I doing now that is good and could be continued/expanded?

What great ideas that work for others could I borrow?

What is my favorite time of the school day? What am I doing differently then? Could I expand or use it in other contexts? Which side of Chart 1.4 am I on?

Chart 1.4   You

Problem-Focused	Solutioning-Focused
Burned(ing) out	Enjoyment
Frustrated	Hopeful
Doubts	Self-esteem
Coping skills	Visions
Stuck	Growing
Surviving	Creating

Destination Discipline

Marie was a teacher I worked with who had been very successful in college and as a mother. Her self-confidence, however, was beginning to wane as her seventh-grade classes continued to be undisciplined despite years of trying every discipline program she could learn about. As we talked, I found out that she would learn a program and follow it to the letter. She had tried token economies, behavior modification, assertive discipline, in-school suspensions, and contracts, to name a few. Although she had done just what the books/workshops said she should do, she explained, she felt like a robot going through the motions, and the students just didn't respond. Instead of discussing why these programs didn't work, I began to question Marie on what did work, (as a successful student, as a capable mother, and some of the time in class now). As we talked, I kept listening for Marie's abilities, pointing out that she seemed to be a good learner herself and that she had amazing desire and determination to be a good teacher. While answering my questions, she began to see her own strengths. Her demeanor changed completely. After a few conversations, Marie began to see that she had the abilities to run a well-disciplined, structured home, that she cared a lot about her students, and that she was ready to try some things in her classroom that had worked with her own children at home. A few weeks later, Marie came to me, full of confidence, relating how she had been interacting so differently with her students—as herself, not as a robot acting out a textbook of interventions. Marie shared that her students were reacting differently to her, more genuinely, and seemed to be trying harder in class.

By looking within herself, being herself, and relying on her own strengths and talents, Marie was able to create an atmosphere of learning in her class. She began seeing students differently as well—not as problems needing fixing or controlling with the latest program, but as capable children whom she cared about and wanted to teach. Marie was using a solutioning focus. Notice there are no specific plans for the worst student or new rules to add to her list. The answers are not laid out in black and white in a manual you can follow, but are individualized with each student.

The solutions, the answers, and the abilities are within you, within your students, and within their parents. Learning how to look, how to see, and how to use them is what solutioning is all about. Start packing your bags of personal potentials, skills, and abilities (see MASTER 3 "Reflection: You"). Then you will be ready to blend in and actualize solutioning with students.

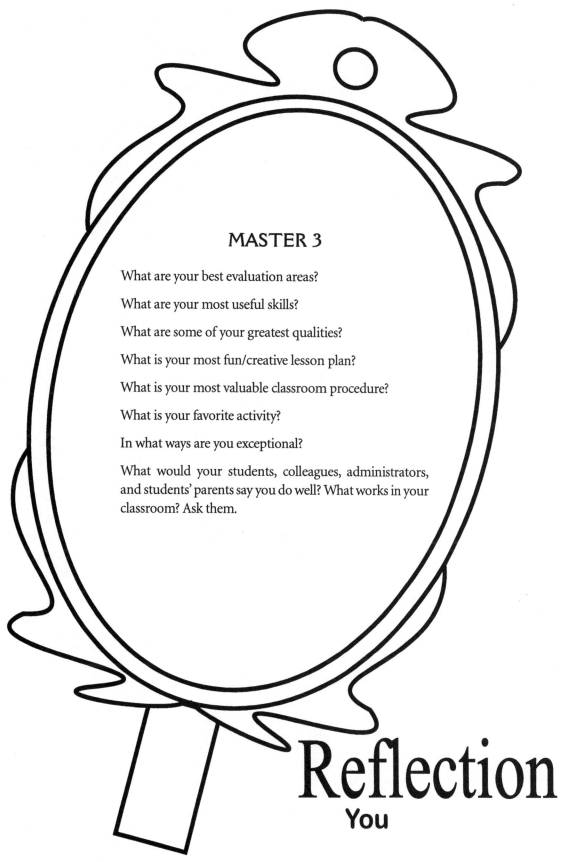

MASTER 3

What are your best evaluation areas?

What are your most useful skills?

What are some of your greatest qualities?

What is your most fun/creative lesson plan?

What is your most valuable classroom procedure?

What is your favorite activity?

In what ways are you exceptional?

What would your students, colleagues, administrators, and students' parents say you do well? What works in your classroom? Ask them.

Reflection
You

Our Journey   *Solutioning can happen as a whole or in parts.*

In Figure 1.1 you will find the Journey Through Solutioning Map, a visual overview of the 3-P process. The map is designed as a framework within which to learn the language, rather than as a procedure to be rigidly followed. In the next four chapters, you will journey through solutioning with the map as a guide, learning the language of the 3-Ps (purpose, potentials, plan) and then follow through with progress. Focus on one chapter at a time, sampling most of the language and intervention ideas, or choose a few questions/phrases that feel good from each chapter and try some complete solutioning conversations. Language Lessons, practices, and student worksheets are supplied to facilitate whichever way you learn best. Remember, solutioning can happen as a whole or in parts. One sentence may start a change in thinking for a student, but it may not be visible for several days. Instating a few phrases/questions into whole-class interactions may positively prevent problems, and complete 3-P conferences will create answers, solutions, and responsible change. Approach the process with an open, flexible mind and remember: "Once you know what works, DO MORE OF IT!" (Carpenter, 1997, p. 117).

Chapter 1 Focused   *Empower every interaction with responsibility*
                                   and ability by using solutioning.

Are you ready to get rid of the responsibility of telling students what to do and what the answers are and of trying to control an entire class? In schools these days, we are asked to do more with more students in less time. Are you tired of looking for causes of problems that only give a chance for blame and no plan for the future? Are you ready to save time while creating a more disciplined environment, enhancing critical thinking, decision-making skills, self-esteem, and lifelong problem-solving abilities? Are you ready to focus on and do more of what works? Then empower every interaction with responsibility and ability by using solutioning.

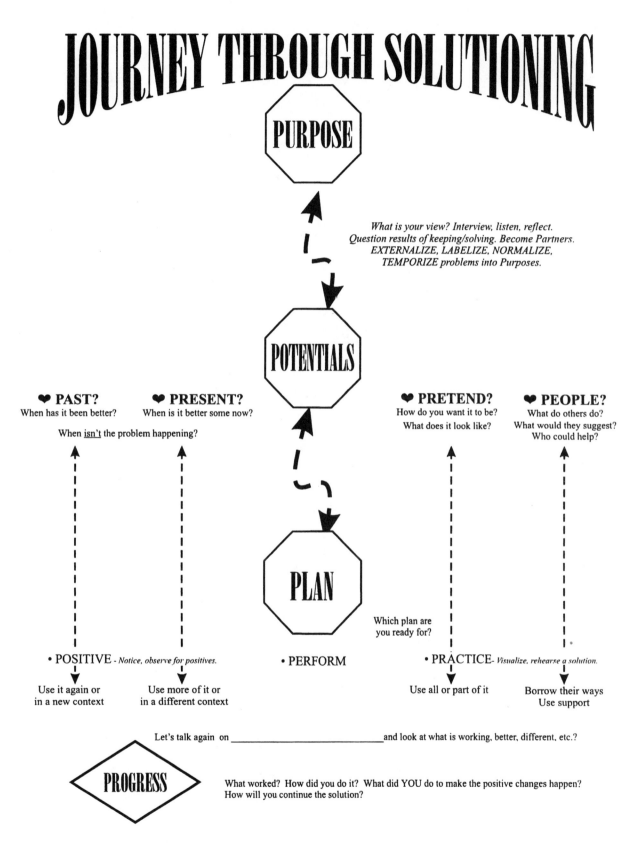

JOURNEY THROUGH SOLUTIONING

PURPOSE

What is your view? Interview, listen, reflect.
Question results of keeping/solving. Become Partners.
EXTERNALIZE, LABELIZE, NORMALIZE,
TEMPORIZE problems into Purposes.

POTENTIALS

❤ **PAST?**
When has it been better?

When <u>isn't</u> the problem happening?

❤ **PRESENT?**
When is it better some now?

❤ **PRETEND?**
How do you want it to be?
What does it look like?

❤ **PEOPLE?**
What do others do?
What would they suggest?
Who could help?

PLAN

Which plan are
you ready for?

• **POSITIVE** - *Notice, observe for positives.*

• **PERFORM**

• **PRACTICE** - *Visualize, rehearse a solution.*

Use it again or
in a new context

Use more of it or
in a different context

Use all or part of it

Borrow their ways
Use support

Let's talk again on _____ and look at what is working, better, different, etc.?

PROGRESS

What worked? How did you do it? What did YOU do to make the positive changes happen?
How will you continue the solution?

Figure 1.1. Journey Through Solutioning Map.

Willyn H. Webb, *The Educator's Guide to Solutioning.* Copyright © 1999 by Corwin Press, Inc.

2

Journey Through Solutioning
Purpose

By helping students see problems as outside themselves, as normal,
temporary, and solvable, powerful and motivating change begins.

The flexibility of solutioning begins with the purpose (see Journey Through Solutioning Map in Figure 2.1). Solutioning brings individualization, now standard in effective instruction, to all interactions by allowing educators and students to begin together, wherever that may be (problem or desire), and form a joint purpose. With a few questions/phrases and using some or all of the solutioning techniques in this chapter, the teacher can initiate a hopeful, motivating, individualized process.

It seems that in the hurried world of education, the purpose, or reason behind the interaction, is often brushed over, assumed, or given, rather than used to make the entire process more productive. It only takes a minute to make a difference with a positive start, not because you spend a lot of time with students wallowing in the mud, complaining, blaming, and engaging in problem talk, but because the view of, the thinking about, or the frame of reference concerning the problem has a huge influence on the outcome or solution (de Shazer, 1985; Metcalf, 1995; O'Hanlon & Weiner-Davis, 1989; Walter & Peller, 1992).

By helping students see problems as outside themselves, as normal, temporary, and solvable, powerful and motivating change begins. It is so rewarding to see the relief on students' faces when they realize that *they* are not the problems. As students begin to view their problems with a solutioning focus, as in the following example, it's like a weight has been lifted. In fact, by using the solutioning language in this chapter, you and your students may no longer have problems to solve at all.

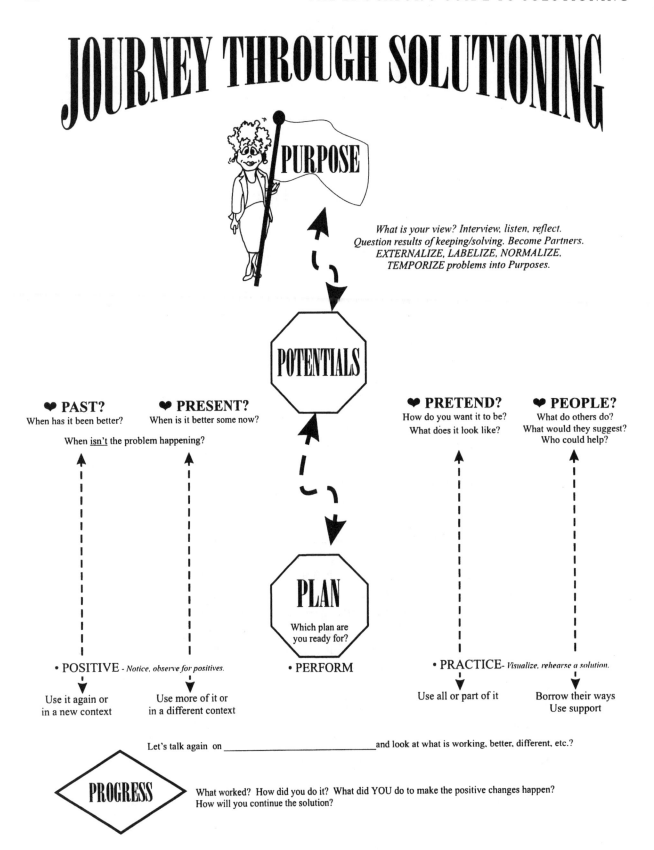

Figure 2.1. Journey Through Solutioning Map.

Willyn H. Webb, *The Educator's Guide to Solutioning.* Copyright © 1999 by Corwin Press, Inc.

Lisa

Lisa, a second-grader, had a speech problem—trouble making the sounds of *r* and *th*. I'll always remember the comment she made after a solutioning conversation. Her eyes brightened, she sat up tall, and nearly jumping out of her chair, she said, "I don't have to talk this way fo evea. I could be like da oda kids." In no time at all, Lisa, now free from the burden of her speech pattern, was seeing herself as more normal. She realized she was a person, not a speech problem. Lisa relaxed, made friends, and gained more self-confidence. Her speech pattern soon corrected itself.

Read through Chart 2.1. Imagine the conversation likely to follow the various starts. Which would you prefer? How about students?

Chart 2.1   Purpose

Problem-Focused	Traditional
"You are a real problem . . ."	"What is your view of this?"
"The problem is . . ."	"Let's find a solution together."
"This has got to change. You are going to . . ."	"What reasons do you have for finding a solution?"
"This is the way it's going to be from now on . . ."	"How do you want things to be?"
"You will do exactly what I tell you to do."	"Let's fight this problem together."
Adversaries	Partners
Telling	Sharing
Control	Responsibility
One-sided communication	Two-way communication

Establish a purpose that is realistic, individualized, and forward moving.

Purpose, Not Problem

The language of solutioning is used to prevent or solve the very problems this chapter talks about manipulating. The simple use of the term *purpose*, rather than *problem*, often eliminates creating one. Sometimes a concern, a need, or a desire require solutioning. So why make these problems by referring to them as such, as in most programs (e.g., Campbell, 1995; Gootman, 1997)? By focusing on, or referring to, a problem, you are more likely to be/become/solidify one. The view held about a problem can open or close solution options. Solutioning moves away from problems and problem talk by establishing a purpose that is realistic, individualized, and forward moving. Very simply, the purpose is the reason for the interaction, whatever that might individually be. The checklist in MASTER 4 "Educator Helpsheet: Purpose" will serve as a guide, both as you learn the tools of this chapter and as you embark on solutioning conversations with students. Remember, this may be all it takes.

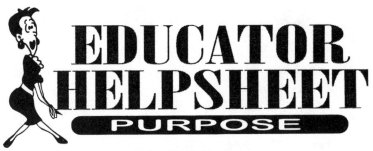

MASTER 4

Information gathering, sharing worldviews, partnering:

Interview—Listen—Reflect

What is your definition of the purpose? What is the student's?

_____

_____

_____

Have you empowered the purpose by considering consequences, results, possibilities of:

Maintaining the problem?   Solving the problem?

_____   _____

_____   _____

_____   _____

_____   _____

Checklist

If necessary, have you . . . ?

externalized _____

labelized _____

temporized _____

normalized _____

What is the co-/re-created, agreed-on description of the purpose?

_____

_____

_____

Building a foundation by manipulating the problem and discussing/creating the purpose sets up a partnership and creates a solvable idea of the situation. Forming partnerships is as simple as eliciting students' input, listening to their points of view, and illustrating care, commitment, and an assumption that a solution will be found together. The initial statements or questions or both of solutioning let students know that the educator is on their side regardless of what the problem might be. This can happen quickly and simply with one carefully worded question or reflection.

Many programs discuss building relationships with students, which are wonderful and very helpful when solutioning. Let's face it, however; in today's world, having a true relationship with every student is sometimes impossible. When you see 180 students per day in 6 rushed class periods, or have many students who speak different languages or have huge ability gaps, or teach five different subjects, and on and on, it is difficult to form relationships with each student. What educators do have with all of their students are *interactions*. Solutioning is a means for a positive, productive interaction, with a relationship as a frequent by-product.

Three skills can quickly be used to build understanding, motivation, and trust into the solutioning partnership. *Interviewing, listening,* and *reflecting* show students that you are with them, give insight into their worldviews, and begin the solutioning process. If you think your partnerships with students need some work or have been caught up in a disciplinary/controlling stance, brushing up on these basics will build a foundation to make the most out of the solutioning language to come.

Interviewing

Interviewing is done by simply encouraging students to share their ideas of the purpose or problem circumstances—for example, "Tell me about being tardy from your point of view." Asking feeling questions, such as "How does that make you feel?" helps students relate their worldviews. By getting students to the feeling level, they will gain greater understanding and be open to sharing. Emotions, thoughts, and behaviors all interact with each other. Sometimes it is difficult for students to get past their current feelings and to think about solutions and behaviors. Providing a minute for the facts and feelings early on often enables students to think more clearly and to feel more positive during the exploration of exceptions and potential solutions to come.

The next two skills of listening and reflecting need to be used in conjunction with the interview for students to feel truly heard, understood, and ready to go as valuable contributors. The comparison of statements in Chart 2.2 will get you started opening solution possibilities, rather than closing them. Notice that none of the solutioning questions mention a problem. Remember, we do not want to create a self-fulfilling prophecy by asking about a problem, thereby labeling/creating one.

Chart 2.2   Solution Possibilities

Close Down	*Open Up*
"I don't care whose problem this is."	"Tell me how you see things."
"It is going to stop right now."	"What is your view?"
"Because I said so."	"What do you think about this?"
"You better shape up now."	"How are you feeling right now?"
"Now you listen to me."	"Do you think a solution would be helpful/
"This is the way things are going to be from	beneficial?"
now on."	"What are your reasons for talking with me?"
"Pay attention."	"What is your point of view?"
"Don't talk to me in that tone of voice."	"What happened in your opinion?"
"Your behavior is not acceptable."	"What do you see as the important facts?"
"The rules are for a reason."	"What purpose might you have for making things
"You will straighten up or I'm sending you to	better?"
the office."	

Listening

After working with their case study students during my course, my adult students termed "mouth control" an important aspect of *listening*. As adults and especially as educators in the habit of giving out knowledge and information, instructing, disciplining, telling, controlling, and so on, we often clearly see solutions, steps that need to be taken, and answers for students. In solutioning, wherein we are giving students responsibility, it is important to hold off our input or instruction until the right time. To listen to students, we have to put aside our own perceptions for a moment and attempt to understand theirs. This is where holding back, or mouth control, is necessary. By concentrating on hearing what students are saying and understanding the emotions, we will be better able to facilitate the solution process.

They Never Cease to Amaze Us

Sent in by a workshop participant

Sara stayed after class on her own and was obviously upset. I was also upset. Sara was easily the brightest girl in class, but lately she had shut down. Her previously perfect grades were fast becoming Cs and Ds. I had attempted to talk with Sara during class, but she had resisted and become angry. I had offered tutoring, more time on assignments, and homework helpers, all of which she had refused. I was glad Sara had chosen to stay, but when I asked Sara what was going on, her answer surprised me. She said that I was picking on her and that I didn't like her. This really threw me because I had previously enjoyed teaching and interacting with her. Sara did talk with her friends or whoever she was sitting by more often than expected. Lately, I had come to realize that she was a leader; if I reprimanded or reminded Sara to be quiet, the others would follow.

Rather than defend myself with that insight, I asked Sara what made her feel picked on or disliked and then just listened. She said that anytime I talked to her, she felt singled out. She said it was just like her stepfather, who was constantly on her and loved to embarrass her in front of others. In fact, it seemed that any comment made directly to Sara, positive or negative, made her feel on-the-spot. As I listened, I began to see that her perception of my joy in interacting with such a bright student was that I was trying to put her on the spot and embarrass her. Even the compliments I often had for Sara were taken as embarrassments. By simply listening, I got into Sara's worldview. I could see how devastating her experience with being singled out had been and how I was contributing to it. So we came up with a plan that Sara would use her outstanding leadership skills to help the group stay focused in class, I would write Sara notes for compliments, and we could interact after class once a week. It turned out that Sara loved the intellectual interaction as well, just not in front of everybody. Within 2 weeks, Sara was turning in all of her assignments, her grades were on their way to As, and we were sharing a wonderful class experience from both our worldviews.

Our perception, as was Sara's, is our reality. This seems especially true with young people. Have you ever asked your class what happened during a fight at lunch? Because of this perceptual, individual reality, listening becomes an invaluable tool when solutioning with students. In our hurried up, self-centered world of educator-authority, our response usually begins to form well before students are finished speaking. Our entire society is answering before listening. It has not always been that way:

> Not too long ago, before our ears became accustomed to an increasing barrage of stimulation, many people knew how to listen attentively while tracking an animal or hearing the approach of rain—or sitting in council with a group of peers. When we are graced with that kind of listening and devoted to its practice, our ability to be empathic grows and we enter a world in which decisions are made by discovery and recognition. (Zimmerman & Coyle, 1991, p. 80)

Where listening was once a matter of survival, it now seems avoided. Are we afraid that if we stop talking we will no longer be teaching? While practicing listening (mouth control), my adult students found that old habits are difficult to break. Even with awareness and effort, they were sometimes too quick to jump in with their own, seemingly better ideas, the answers, the right way, the correction, the reward, the punishment, and on and on before giving students a chance truly to process and answer the solutioning questions. The interaction becomes one-sided, and the partnership suffers. Solutioning is an interaction based on joint sharing where potentials are explored and plans are created on the basis of students' input. Let's not just humor our students by asking for their input and then not really listening when they share. This could be more detrimental than anything else. If we ask for sharing, input, opinions, exceptional times, potentials, visions, we then have to listen to them when offered.

Don't think that actively, attentively listening to students during solutioning conversations will increase the time required. It seems that solutions are created, constructed, and discovered more quickly with a little more listening and a little less telling, not to mention the success rate in carrying them out. Which are you more likely to do—use your own good idea or do what someone else has told you to do? Students are no different. Let's listen and hear them so that they can own their solutions. Otherwise, who has the responsibility? Otherwise, who will listen—drug dealers, gangs, smooth talkers who want to have sex?

Reflecting

Whether or not you agree with students' opinions or feelings, *reflecting* them builds trust in the partnership. After listening just enough, a quick, simple sentence often lets students know they have been heard and understood—for example, "That must be really frustrating to do your homework and then lose it." Students are not used to hearing this type of response from educators. The more typical response seems to go something like this: "Well, if you would put it in your book (clean your locker, organize your notebook, etc.), maybe you would remember it." The difference in the two example statements may just open or close solution possibilities from the student's point of view. Do not let students go on and on with lots of complaining, blaming, and moaning. Let them complain just long enough for you to be able to reflect back accurately their meanings and feelings. This will help them vent a little and help you get into their worldviews, show that you care, and partner up. As Allen Mendler (1992) states, "By accepting people as they are, we make it possible for them to risk change" (p. 36). A strong foundation can be built in a very short time. This is especially necessary if the situation is an emotional one for a student. Be wary of reflecting/supporting blaming and excuses. Find the feeling to reflect, not the excuse.

Take a moment and review reflective listening in MASTER 5 "Practice Makes Perfect: Building a Strong Foundation." This skill can be practiced with a partner, who chooses an issue or feeling to tell you about. You will interview, listen, and reflect. Your partner could give you feedback with a thumbs up or thumbs sideways (not down) signal. Most of you use these skills on a regular basis already. Rehearsal may help you apply them even with the most frustrating students as you embark on your solutioning experience together. Sometimes this is all it takes, as Gary S. Heller (1996), principal of Monroe-Woodbury Senior High School in Central Valley, New York, points out:

"[T]he key to a successful intervention with a particular student is his or her understanding and realization that someone, finally, really listened." (p. 5)

Practice Makes Perfect

BUILDING A STRONG FOUNDATION

MASTER 5

INTERVIEW: Ask the student about her or his view of the situation. Gain insight into her or his worldview. Use an open question to begin: "Tell me about being tardy from your viewpoint." Then clarify with closed questions about specifics if needed: "Do you have an alarm clock?" "How do you get to school?" Encourage the student to share feelings about the situation: "How does it make you feel when you are tardy so often?"

LISTEN: Really hear the information, meaning, and feelings the student is sharing. Give her or him a moment to talk without you interrupting, instructing, or directing. Paraphrase or summarize quickly so that the student believes she or he has been heard: "You wake up on time, but then many events happen during your morning that often make you late to school."

REFLECT: Reflect feeling and meaning so that the student feels understood. Observe the student's emotions and feed key feelings and meanings back. This does not mean you have to agree: "So you think the other students hate you. That must make it hard for you to come to school. You feel frustrated when your mom can't drive you to school."

Practice reflecting with the following statement:

> *I hate having so many zeros. I don't want to get an F on my report card. I don't know what happens; sometimes I just don't do the assignments or I forget or I lose them. My parents are going to kill me if I get an F. I've never gotten an F before. I used to get pretty good grades.*

Paraphrase the essence of what the student has said and add affective, or feeling, words that are in tune with the student's emotional experience.

_____

_____

_____

_____

(Remember not to give any suggestions, reprimands, or instructions as this point; just feed back the highlights and the feelings.)

The student may have expressed some feelings (explicit feelings), and others may be unexpressed, hidden, or only communicated through nonverbals (implicit feelings). Try to cover both in your reflective statement.

Explicit feelings: _____

Implicit feelings:_____

(continued)

MASTER 5 Continued

Now try reflecting feeling and meaning with this statement:

I hate school. I'm miserable the whole time I'm here. The teachers suck, and the kids are jerks. The only reason I come is because my mom makes me. I'm not doing this assignment. I could care less.

_____

_____

_____

_____

(This statement could have different meanings for different students [e.g., the work is too hard, she or he doesn't have any friends, she or he is angry with you or another teacher]. By reflecting your impression of the student's meaning and feelings, you will be able to check out your observations and communicate that you know what's going on.)

Sometimes students are reluctant to share information and feelings, especially in a problem situation. Even this type of resistance can be reflected to build a stronger relationship.

I don't know what the problem is or how I feel. Just leave me alone.

_____

_____

_____

_____

Did your reflection involve something like this: "So, you feel as if you don't want to care about what happens and talking about this is so upsetting that you'd rather avoid it?" Showing the student that you understand how she or he feels encourages the student to open up a little more. After this, you could go on with the solutioning conversation. After examining some exceptions, the student usually has a more positive affect.

To reflect feeling and meaning in a way that the student feels heard and understood, you need a vocabulary of feeling words and emotional labels that students will identify with. It may be helpful to begin generating a list of possible feeling words for use with the age level of your students. Don't forget different intensities of the same emotion—for example, *annoyed, mad, furious.*

_____	_____	_____	_____
_____	_____	_____	_____
_____	_____	_____	_____
_____	_____	_____	_____

You may also need to assist students in naming their own feelings. Sometimes pictures are worth a thousand words. Try the faces and feelings on the following page.

FEELING FACES

Establishing a   *Focusing on the positive, the solution, and the*
Joint Purpose   *future facilitates change in the desired direction.*

In dealing with people (students, parents, colleagues), no two participants or their situations are alike. Circumstances where you both come to solutioning motivated to solve the problem are ideal and, in schools today, rare. In the initial stages (**purpose, potentials**) of the solutioning conversation, a joint **purpose** must be established.

During some solutioning interactions, students share a **purpose** (whatever that might individually be) and are eager to find solutions. Some students acknowledge a problem/need/desire, own it, and are motivated to create a **plan** to solve/achieve it. In these cases, very little time is spent on the **purpose,** and the conversation moves right into an exploration of the exceptions to the problem and **potential** solutions: "Focusing on the positive, the solution, and the future facilitates change in the desired direction. Therefore, focus on solution-oriented talk rather than on problem-oriented talk" (Walter & Peller, 1992, p. 37).

We do not always have the luxury of having students who see a problem/need, have a **purpose,** and choose to seek help in solving/achieving it. A wonderful conversation could take place between student and teacher during which many **potential** solutions are discussed but the solution does not happen because the student did not feel the need to solve the problem (share the **purpose**). In fact, the student may not even have thought a problem existed at all. Some students attend school for the social aspects alone, some students do outstanding jobs of coping, and others seem just not to care. These students do not own their problem or see a need to solve it. They may think it is the teacher's problem, their parents' problem, the other students, their ADD, or some other excuse. They have no **purpose.** In the following sections, we discuss problems, but only in ways designed to take away their influence, establish a joint **purpose,** and motivate solutions.

Solutioning enables educators and students to buy into a **purpose** for finding a solution in a validating and motivating way. In discussing motivation, Madeline Hunter (1967) uses the example of "Sally who was majoring in boys and perfectly contented to ignore the trivia of a math paper" (p. 9). Sound familiar? It is very unlikely that a student like Sally would join the solutioning team and readily agree that boys were a problem and math more important. Establishing a **purpose** that Sally agrees with is an important first step for success. Telling Sally that math is more important won't work. In fact, I bet that somewhere, sometime, someone has probably tried to get that message across. Using the questions of solutioning, Sally will be able to find her own reasons and abilities for doing her math. She will be more motivated and cooperative as a result. As one of my adult students commented,

It is so nice to adopt the solutioning focus and no longer feel the burden of trying to *make* students do things or *convince* them of the value. We are educators, not salespeople. It is much more enjoyable to work with students co-discovering through questioning rather than giving sales pitches, and students appreciate the responsibility. (Dottie Miller, principal)

The first step is to enable Sally to realize the need and to empower her to solve her problem. So far, this has been everyone else's problem but hers. She needs choice and responsibility in order to establish ownership.

Educator: Sally, why do you think I called you in today?

Sally: Because you're mad that I don't do my work.

Educator: I want to know how you feel about not doing your work. (interviewing)

Sally: I feel like I'm tired of you and my parents hassling me about it. It seems like someone is always on my back. I just want to be left alone.

Educator: That sounds like an awful way to feel. (reflecting feeling) What would happen if everyone left you alone? (questioning for consequences)

Sally: **(after a long pause)** Well, if I didn't do my work, I would flunk math and maybe get held back, or I would decide for myself to do enough of it to pass.

Educator: Wow, you really considered all the possibilities. (validating her answer) Which do *you*, not I or your parents, want to have happen—flunk or pass? (clarifying and questioning for further consequences)

Sally: I want to pass. It would be embarrassing to get an F, and I'd just die if I got held back and my friends went on.

Educator: That sounds as if it would be devastating for you. It's cool that *you've decided that you want to pass.* (restating—establishing **purpose**)

Now a partnership can be formed to help her achieve *her* **purpose**, which just so happens to be the educator's and her parents' too, of passing math. Sally is no longer resisting being controlled, but is taking control. She is able to take control because she was given choice in establishing her **purpose** through the language of solutioning. (Even if Sally had chosen to fail, the result would have been the same as what her current behavior was leading to anyway.) The chance taken in giving her choice was really risk-free. Now **potential** solutions can be explored and a **plan** for passing math created. The time it would take to have this conversation is far less than the time that would be required for daily badgering, telephone calls home, and/or poor progress reports each week.

With the underlying qualities of choice and responsibility, students gain hope and motivation through the use of only a few techniques. The reluctant student, however, may think that change would mean surrender. This form of "reaction" may require the use of many of the techniques in this chapter and even a look at **potentials** (Chapter 3) before the student is ready and willing to find a solution. It is for these students that so many language options and techniques are included. This may make the conversation seem long or complicated, which it is not.

Remember, change is not always obvious at first. A change in thinking or feeling (neither of which is always initially observable) may occur with the first solutioning experience when the student begins to see the problem as external from the self, more normal or temporary, and most of all, more solvable. When that happens, the student will often come back to you later, ready to move on and to consider potential solutions. The partner approach and the forward, positive focus of solutioning will help even the most unwilling student feel more hopeful, which grows into motivation for change.

Empower With Purpose

Many aspects of discipline, like the consequences of not solving the problem, are included in solutioning and may be discussed in detail: school policies, rules, punishments and other natural consequences. In solutioning, however, instead of disciplining (in most programs, the educator imposes consequences on students), you simply question students about their views of the consequences that are likely if the problem is continued and the consequences that are likely if/when the problem is solved. This allows students the opportunity to process the entire spectrum of possibilities and to make choices. Students gain a sense of control over their situations and are motivated to join in solutioning.

Choice and control encourage taking responsibility—what we usually expect students to learn by doing exactly what we tell them. In our telling, we rarely have students consider the possible results of solving, of not having the problem, being in trouble, feeling upset, and so on and what will be different then. This takes them toward what they do want (solution) instead of what they don't want (punishment). Having a **purpose** and working toward a better tomorrow takes power away from problems and gives it (and responsibility) to students.

We all can think of times when choice did not seem like an option: The student had to comply with the rules or fail, or be expelled, or whatever. The consequences/results often have a greater effect when presented to students as a choice, rather than when inflicted by some authority. Being up front and discussing the possible results/consequences of continuing with a problem avoids the cat-and-mouse game we sometimes play with students who are sneaky—not trying to correct behavior, just figuring out how not to get caught or pushing to see just how far they can go. Use the possible results, both positive and negative, to be proactive together with forward, purposeful thinking. Even when a problem behavior persists and a negative consequence (punishment) happens, the anger/resentment/disappointment that students feel is more likely to be turned inward. Students who feel punished by authority are angry with authority and give little thought to the part they played in their circumstances, which is not responsibility.

Why not use consequences for all they are worth by setting up students to engage in some self-examination and reflection about the problem and solutioning to solve it, rather than contemplating how to outsmart or get revenge on the teacher/principal/parent? The following case study illustrates the value of choice in guiding students away from a problem-oriented to a purposeful, solution-oriented view of their situation.

The Telephone Call

Adapted from a workshop participant's story "Phone Call"

Jerry (a seventh-grader): You're going to call my mom, aren't you? I knew you'd do that.

Educator (with an initial solutioning question): What is our **purpose** for being here right now?

Jerry: So you can call my mom and get me in trouble.

Educator: It sounds as if you are really worried about your mom getting called. Whether I call or not, why are we here? (reflecting, questioning for a **purpose**)

Jerry: Because you want to get me in a lot of trouble.

Educator: What brought us in here today? (questioning for a **purpose**)

Jerry: You caught me writing on the wall, and now you're gonna give me detention and call my mom to get me in trouble.

Educator: Who wrote on the wall?

Jerry: I did.

Educator: What do the school rules say about writing on the wall and what happens if you do? (questioning for consequences)

Jerry: I don't know.

Educator: Here, I'll let you look at them. They say that if you write on the wall, you have to spend detention cleaning them. Does it say anything in there about me getting you in trouble?

Jerry: No.

Educator: Who broke the rules and got you in trouble?

Jerry: I guess I did.

Educator: What happens when you are tempted to do something against the rules but don't? (questioning for positive consequences, building **potentials**)

Jerry: I was gonna ditch with some friends last week but knew if my mom found out, she'd kill me, so I said no and went to class. They got caught and got ISS and I didn't.

Educator: Great! Sounds like *you have the ability to make a decision to follow the rules.* Which decision feels better? Which keeps your mom from getting called? (questioning for positive consequences) When you make more of those types of decisions from now on, things will be different, huh? (assuming solution, building toward a **plan**)

Jerry: Yeah, it's not that hard. I know how to stay out of trouble. It isn't worth it. I hate detention, and my mom is going to kill me.

Educator: So, what's your **plan?**

Jerry: Make the right decision, like before.

Educator: Let's talk in a week. I want to hear about all the good things that happen when you are making the right decisions. OK?

Mom was called (by Jerry) to explain his need for a ride after detention. He felt as if he had made a bad decision and had to pay the price, not angry with me. More important, he left with a solution, a **plan** to achieve more positive experiences from now on. The rules could have just been imposed, Jerry made to suffer the consequences, and the situation ended there. Experience shows, however, that repeat offenses are more likely when the goal becomes outsmarting a detested teacher, rather than making the right decision to stay out of trouble. With a few quick questions, Jerry was able to look at the problem with a new perspective and thus complete the solutioning process.

Try the questions in MASTER 6 "Language Lesson: Empower." Have a col- league, spouse, or someone else play the role of the resistive student and get the feel of asking. Set up sample situations that are typical of your current students and do a quick role-play. Get feedback on how it felt to be asked and to respond. As you become more comfortable with the language, make a copy and have it handy when a problem arises with a student in class or use MASTER 7 "Student Worksheet: Empower With Purpose" (together or individually).

Empower

MASTER 6

Establish a joint **purpose** for finding solutions by helping the student explore the results of continuing with the problem or solving it. Do not impose consequences. Your input should be in an information-giving way when the student does not know possible outcomes.

What will be different/better when this problem is solved?

What will happen if you choose to maintain the problem?

What was/is better about times when you did not have the problem?

If you continue to _____ (e.g., lose your papers, get in fights, come in late), what will happen? At home? At school? How will that feel?

When you start _____ (e.g., turning in your papers getting along, being on time), what will be different/better? At home? At school? With friends?

What might I say are some reasons why solutioning would be helpful?

What reasons might your _____ (e.g., parents, teacher, friends) have for wanting you to have _____(e.g., better grades, fewer detentions)?

What benefits will you experience when you solve this problem?

What do the school rules say about this?

How do you feel now? How will you feel when the problem is solved?

For now, don't try to change anything. Maintain your problem and notice the consequences.

Tell me about your future **plans.** Is there room for (the problem)?

Who will be thfe first to notice when the problem is solved?

SOURCE: Questions adapted from *Solutioning: Solution-Focused Interventions for Counselors* (pp. 54-55), by W. Webb, 1999, Philadelphia: Taylor and Francis/Accelerated Development. Used with permission.

Add your own on the back of this sheet:

LANGUAGE LESSON

Empower With Purpose

MASTER 7

Consider what will happen if you continue to have the problem OR what will happen when you use a solution.

What if you . . . ?

Maintain/Keep the Problem	*Solve the Problem*
_____	_____
_____	_____
_____	_____
_____	_____
_____	_____
_____	_____
_____	_____
_____	_____
_____	_____
_____	_____

What do you want to do? Are you ready to find a solution?

Externalize

*Resistance is lessened and cooperation encouraged when
the problem is a something, not a someone, not each other.*

Think for a moment of the most difficult class you've ever had to teach. Now answer this question: What was the problem? If you are like most educators, the names of a few students popped into your head. On days when one or more of those "problem" students were absent, the class was so much more manageable, right? Unfortunately, you cannot transfer those students out of your class, you cannot arrange for them to move away, and snuffing them out is out of the question. You can work with them, however, by building and expanding on the times when they are behaving, when the class is more manageable, and when things are working. With a solutioning focus, those problem students are no longer the problems. In fact, this change in the way you view them may affect the way you react to them and, in turn, the way they react with you. The change has already begun, and you've not spoken a single word. Solutioning works toward creating more of the better, acceptable, tolerable times. Behaviors, thoughts, feelings, and actions, not people, are the problems. In solution-focused brief therapy, this is called "externalizing the problem" (O'Hanlon & Beadle, 1994; Webb, 1999; White & Epston, 1990).

When a problem is externalized, it ceases feeling like such a burden. Problems begin to reflect what students want/need to change, manage, or control in their lives. Resistance is lessened and cooperation encouraged when the problem is a something, not a someone, not each other.

With an externalized problem, the effects of the problem on everyone involved can be shared, empathy increased, and teamwork established. Everyone feels empowered when she or he can step outside the problem and feel a new sense of control. The partnership is now formed, and the opponent is the problem. Externalizing is especially useful in the following circumstances:

- The student feels as if she or he is the problem.
- The student blames someone else (maybe the educator).
- The student believes that the educator sees her or him as the problem.
- The student and the educator battle each other.
- The problem being solved needs clarification.

Notice how quickly students catch on to an externalized problem in the following case study example.

The Chatterbox

Soraya was a fifth-grade student who enjoyed the social aspects of school tremendously. As her health teacher, I often observed how difficult it was for her to switch from lunchtime social topics to fifth-grade health topics. Her talking not only made it difficult for me to get the class on-task but also affected her in many ways: causing her to feel like a problem student, to be reprimanded and disciplined, and to receive lower grades than her abilities would suggest. After I had used the solutioning focus to view Soraya and the "talking" in this way, I was prepared to have a solutioning conversation with her. I asked Soraya to stay after class one afternoon when the talking had been especially bothersome for both of us. My goal was to help Soraya see how the talking controlled and affected her. My fear was that she would feel in trouble or lectured. The questions used were adapted from suggestions by Linda Metcalf, a solution-focused author (1995), for beginning a discussion when a student is sent to the office.

Educator: What might I say is the reason why I asked you in today?

Soraya: You're mad at me, and I'm in trouble for talking all of the time.

Two important points that needed to be addressed came out in her answer. First, *she* was feeling like a problem, as if I were angry with *her,* and that *she* was in trouble. Second, she was aware of the problem of talking but had not yet externalized it.

Educator: First of all, I am not mad at *you.* You are right that "talking" is something I want to discuss today. Do you usually know when Talking is disrupting the class?

Soraya replied with a detailed answer of all the times she should be doing her work but instead talks to her group (no matter who is in it). She also described times when I was instructing the class but she remembered something that had happened during lunch and she had to tell her friends. This resulted in a reprimand, a look, and finally a seating change that embarrassed and upset her tremendously. Within this explanation, Soraya, in a small way, began to separate "talking" from herself and to view the behavior and its influence on her. Soraya is examining the *results* of "talking."

Educator: Have you noticed times when Talking doesn't bother you and keep you from being noticed in a negative way?

Soraya: Sometimes when nothing really exciting is going on with my friends, I don't talk as much. I really got into a couple of labs that we've done and forgot to tell my friends stuff. I also know that after a couple of "listens" and bad looks my seat might get moved soon, so I don't talk for the rest of that class period.

Educator: When has this happened before, controlling Talking and keeping it from getting you in trouble?

She named a few times like the ones above where she knew what would come next so she stopped. She also remembered a time when she really wanted to spend the night with friends and didn't want to risk having her parents called by the school and ruining her chances.

Soraya's demeanor changed so much with each new question. The whipped puppy who had walked in knowing she was a problem and in trouble had become a motivated individual teaming up with me against a problem named "Talking."

Educator: If I were to watch you during those times when Talking was not disrupting the class, what do you think I would see you doing?

Soraya: I don't know, just doing my work. I would be looking down at my book more so I didn't see my friends and have to tell them something. I would probably be writing them notes.

Educator: Wow, so you can control Talking, and you know just how: doing you work, looking down, or writing notes.

Soraya brightened and looked almost mighty.

Educator: What will be better when Talking is controlled by you more of the time? Who will notice? What will be in it for you?

Soraya: My friends would notice and think something was wrong or that I was mad at them. You would notice and not tell me to "listen" or embarrass me so much. My parents would probably notice because they wouldn't get calls and because my grades might go up.

Soraya began to feel a sense of power in her ability to control "Talking," thus freeing her from a huge burden. Soraya and I continued by working on a **plan** that basically consisted of Soraya controlling Talking by first letting her friends know what she was doing and why and then using what had worked before more often (doing her work, looking down, listening). We decided she would be able to write one note per class (when absolutely necessary) if it did not affect her or her friends' grades. Soraya tried her **plan** for 3 days before meeting with me again. We had one more conversation during which we noted and celebrated all of the ways she had controlled Talking, what the results were, how she felt about it, and what she would do to continue using her solutions.

By externalizing the problem and making it "Talking," rather than Soraya, **potential** solutions were possible and discussion could take place. After months of trying to reason with her, punishing her, and explaining to her why her talking had to stop (for both of us and her parents), Soraya set a **purpose**, finally took responsibility, and controlled talking. As long as she felt as if she was the problem, her defenses were up, her excuses creative, and her blaming constant. Her self-esteem was being attacked every time she was disciplined for talking. When she realized that talking was controlling her, she was able to switch her defenses away from me and onto talking. We were now partners, and not only did our problem get solved, but we enjoyed a new and wonderful relationship.

The questions used in helping Soraya *externalize* her problem were key. The language used portrayed my solutioning focus and led Soraya in that direction. Notice in the language that "talking" was referred to as something external with a name. Talking was given such qualities as the ability to control and get Soraya in trouble. Soraya was given power over it when she was asked about when she controlled talking. This language illustrated the assumption that Soraya did have that ability, which could be expanded into a **plan.** Bill O'Hanlon (1996) suggests the following ways to use language in externalizing problems. The examples are taken from my classes and workshop participants' input as to how they applied the techniques in their settings.

Name/Personify. Talk to the person or family as if the problem was another person with an identity, will, tactics, and intentions that often have the effect of oppressing, undermining, or dominating the person or family.

For example,

> Are there times when you overcome MAD's desire to get you in a fight and suspended?
>
> What happens differently when SLEEP doesn't win and you get to school on time?
>
> How often does FORGETTING cause you to get a zero?
>
> When doesn't TALKING bother you?

Investigate the Influence of the Problem on the Person. Find out how the person has felt dominated or forced by the problem to do or experience things she or he didn't like. Be careful about using casual terms (*makes, causes, gets*).

For example,

> When has ADD invited you to do something you regretted later?
>
> What subjects does BOREDOM try to make you avoid and then fail?
>
> What happens when CHEATING invites you to look at your neighbor's paper during a test?

Investigate the Influence of the Person on the Problem. Find out about moments of choice or success the person has had in not being dominated or forced by the problem to do or experience things she or he didn't like. Inquire about differences the person has with the problem.

For example,

> Tell me about times when you haven't let YELLING take over.
>
> How does it feel when you beat GRAFFITI and don't get in trouble?
>
> When you win over ANGER and walk away from a fight, what happens?

Use These Moments of Choice or Success as a Gateway to Alternate (Hero) Stories of Identity. Encourage the person or her or his intimates to explain what kind or person this individual is such that she or he had those moments of choice or success.

For example,

> Wow, you are some kind of kid to fight off FORGETTING like that. How do you do that?

> What skills do you use that you can overcome SMOKING and walk away?

> Tell me about your creativity that enables you to overcome BOREDOM and do your homework.

> How do you explain that you are the type of person who could stand up against CONFUSION and ask for help?

Historicize. Find historical evidence explaining how the person was able to stand up to, defeat, or escape from the dominance or oppression of the problem.

For example,

> Last year as a freshman, how were you able to overcome PRESSURE so well?

> In the past, how did you control GUM CHEWING?

Socialize. Find a real or imagined audience for the changes you have been discussing. Enroll the person as an expert consultant on solving or defeating the problem.

For example,

> Who will notice first that BULLYING isn't in your life anymore?

> What would you tell a kindergartner about how to defeat FRUSTRATION successfully in school?

> Who has known you for a long time and could remind you how nice it is when you beat NAME CALLING?

According to Metcalf (1995), "Externalizing problems with adolescents and children helps them see the problems as separate from themselves and see themselves not as failures, but intruded upon" (p. 53). Three additional benefits are discouraging blaming, empowering students, and getting the problem "out there" where teacher and student can fight it, which is very motivating (Webb, 1999). White and Epston (1990) have found the following ways in which externalizing is helpful to persons in their struggle with problems. I added the parenthetical remarks to illustrate the symmetry of my own findings as stated above:

1. Decreases unproductive conflict between persons, including those disputes over who is responsible for the problem (lessens blame)

2. Undermines the sense of failure that has developed for many persons in response to the continuing existence of the problem despite their attempts to resolve it (empowers)

3. Paves the way for persons to cooperate with each other, to unite in a struggle against the problem, and to escape its influence in their lives and relationships (lessens blame, motivates)

4. Opens new possibilities for persons to take actions to retrieve their lives and relationships from the problem and its influence (empowers, motivates)

Most of the students and teachers I talk to think the problem is one person or another. By eliciting some clear thinking to identify the problem itself, blaming can be short-circuited. (Christine Ames, middle-level language arts teacher; used with permission from Christine Ames)

Debbie Ferris found externalizing helpful in working with her case study, Mr. B, who wanted to improve his reading.

Mr. B

Journal entry of Debbie Ferris, elementary special education teacher (Used with permission from Debbie Ferris)

Mr. B has a reading problem and wants to improve. So, we isolated reading as a separate entity and told it to look closer at each word and take its time. He talked to Reading and told it that he had power over it.

It's your turn. Try the suggestions from MASTER 8 "Language Lesson: Externalize" to incorporate externalizing into your own situations. These questions and phrases are different and may feel strange and awkward at first, for both you and your students. The results of ending blaming and excuses, of working with instead of against each other, and of finding solutions are well worth the tongue-tied insecurity you may experience during your first attempts. Then complete MASTER 9 "Practice Makes Perfect: The Externalizer."

I really like the idea of "externalizing the problem" because so many of our youngsters today just want to be liked and accepted. Once we make them realize they are not the problem, but the behavior is, half of the battle is already won. (Kevin Marushack, high school math teacher; used with permission from Kevin Marushack)

Externalize

MASTER 8

Let's fight (name of problem behavior).

Instead of each other, let's battle (name of problem).

Sounds like the problem is _____ (e.g., cheating, lateness, yelling, moving around, goofing, smoking, pinching).

When (name of problem) causes you to get in trouble, how do you feel?

What does (name of problem: e.g., anger, talking, ditching) do to get you in detention, the office, out of recess?

Tell me about times when you have beaten (controlled, overcome) the problem (e.g., fighting, crying) and kept your cool.

How have you stood up to _____ (e.g., teasing, fear, cheating)?

Tell me about your abilities to win over the problem.

What are some reasons to beat (name of problem)?

How often do you overcome (problem's) desire to make you (problem behavior)?

Who will notice first when _____ (e.g., teasing, yelling, zeros) aren't in your life anymore?

Now that you will be turning your back on (problem name), what will be different here at school? At home?

What would you name the problem?

Describe what it is we are finding a solution for.

How is it going to feel when (name) no longer causes problems?

Add your own on the back of this sheet:

SOURCE: Adapted from *Solutioning: Solution-Focused Interventions for Counselors* (pp. 48-50), by W. Webb, 1999, Philadephia: Taylor and Francis/Accelerated Development. Used with permission.

LANGUAGE LESSON

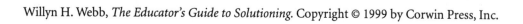

Practice Makes Perfect

THE EXTERNALIZER

MASTER 9

Chart 2.3   Brainstorm what you might say in attempting to help students see common problems as external, as controllable, and as solvable. Take yourself through an imaginary discussion with a student, using phrases from each section. How does it feel to use the language? How might the student react?

Common Student Problems	Name/Personify	Influences Problem on Person	Person on Problem
Example: Fighting	Fighting, Anger Blowing Up	Forces/controls student Gets student in trouble	Reminders help control Avoiding detention Count to ten
Add yours here:			

Common Student Problems	Hero Stories	Historicize	Socialize
Example: Fighting	"Wow, you controlled fighting today. How?"	"Yesterday, you had the power to walk away."	"What would you tell a 1st grader about how to overcome Fighting/ Anger?"
Add yours here:			

Remember Lisa, the student with speech problems at the beginning of this chapter? The thoughts that students have about problems greatly influence the solvability. Sometimes the first and sometimes the only change needed is in how students view the situation. The feelings and the behaviors will follow. Language is a very powerful tool in helping students form a solvable yet realistic view of their problem(s) and create a **purpose**. The problem is still there; however, it is in a more workable/solvable form. The following techniques are very subtle in their manipulation of the language, but the results are anything but subtle. Give them a try and see joint **purposes** formed and change begin.

Labelize

A discussion regarding the influence of labels on children is not new to education. A label often becomes a self-fulfilling prophecy that can have enormous consequences, both positive and negative. Have you ever received your class lists at the beginning of the year and immediately labeled students as ADD, rebellious, shy, slow, hyperactive, brain, trouble maker, dysfunctional family, and so on? Sound familiar? Reacting to students according to their "labels" may affect their behavior. We often live up to others' expectations of us. Metcalf (1995) believes that "the labels we often place on people keep them stuck" (p. 4). Granted, some labels get students special services that are desperately needed and very helpful. Pre-assessments and determining student needs are all necessary components to effective teaching (necessary components can also encourage negative labeling). "Classifying students may give us a means to divide them into appropriate classes, but it can also make us participants in exacerbating problems" (Metcalf, 1995, p. 5).

When thinking about and discussing a **purpose** as in solutioning, it is important to look at the *label,* or the word(s), used. It is up to us to manipulate the power of problems by labelizing them. We can create a positive expectation or a limited fact; we can describe actions or fixed states (Webb, 1999). Using description, which is more action oriented and less fixed, can cast a positive light and begin change (Webb, 1999). Descriptions are more individual, more adaptable, and more solvable than static labels. Labelize with strength-based descriptions to provide ideas for solutions. Do the exercise in MASTER 10 "Practice Makes Perfect: Labelize" to see how it feels to be described by your deficits as compared with by your strengths.

Practice Makes Perfect

LABELIZE

MASTER 10

1. Using educational, pathological, or deficit-based labels and words, describe yourself in 50 words or less.

   (Example) I am a procrastinator. I don't clean up after myself. I am a cheat (on taxes). I eat too much fat and sugar. I am phony to some of my colleagues.

Now it's your turn:

_____

_____

_____

2. Using solutioning-focused, strengths-based descriptive words, describe yourself in 50 words or less.

   (Example) I take really great care of my daughter. I always write out detailed lesson plans. My students know I care about them. I served on the curriculum committee for 2 years.

Now it's your turn:

_____

_____

_____

Ask Yourself: How did each style of introduction feel to you? If you were a student, which would you prefer as a starting point in a relationship? Which pointed out more solution ideas? Could you rewrite the first label-oriented (procrastinator, cheat, phony) version with a solutioning focus?

   (Example) I wait to finish things some of the time. I am honest in most situations but not on taxes. I am aware of my diet flaws and know about good nutrition. I do what I need to do to get along with everyone at school.

Now it's your turn:

_____

_____

_____

Some strengths can even be found in deficits, strengths that make the most logical solutions. Helping students (and ourselves) positively describe, or *labelize*, is one step toward a **purpose,** paving the way toward solution possibilities. Frances Hunt, a master educator of 25 years, labelized so very creatively:

The Ability

Journal entry of Frances Hunt, third-grade teacher (Used with permission from Frances Hunt)

Instead of labeling my student as stubborn or hard headed or angry, I described her as having the "ability" to stay mad for extended periods of time, which takes a lot of perseverance.

Hunt went on to use this ability of perseverance in helping the student get along with the speech teacher and control outbursts.

Labelizing only takes a second and is an easy habit to form. It begins with awareness and ends with a solutioning-focused description. Look at the ideas in Chart 2.4 in MASTER 11 "Language Lesson: Labelize." These are not meant to replace automatically, but rather to encourage you to begin your own process with more hopeful words that fit each unique situation.

Labelize

MASTER 11

Chart 2.4   Think about your class, students you've struggled with in the past, and
common labels in your district, and then try to say the same thing in a
more workable, solvable way. Change connotations and open doors to
explore potential solutions. Change common educational labels to
simpler, everyday descriptions.

Negative Labels	Solutioning Description
ADHD	Energetic sometimes
Emotional	Has strong feelings
Learning disabled	Needs more time
Rebellious	Becoming own person
Lazy	Forgetful sometimes
Limited intelligence	Needs more instruction
Troublemaker	Not successful yet
Talkative	Good communicator
Dysfunctional family	Coping with a lot
Depressed	Sad sometimes
Neglected	Needs some attention
Unmotivated	Not motivated yet
Failure	Not passing yet
Poor reader	Good at math/sports

Now add your own:

LANGUAGE LESSON

So far, the labels referred to have been those placed on students by educators. The labels students give themselves, that parents give them, and that (sometimes worse of all) students give each other are all part of the interactions surrounding problems as well. Challenge these labels through a change in language. This small change can help a problem seem more solvable, leading to a **purpose.**

The labels that students give themselves are the most difficult: "I'm a loser," "I'll never pass," "Nobody will ever like me," "I'm a nerd," "I'm a stoner," "I'm the class clown." Operating with a solutioning focus will enable us to confront these self-imposed labels and lead students toward more hopeful and productive views of themselves and their problems. Replacing these labels with new descriptions, or labelizing them, is done most effectively by the students. It seems that because they gave themselves the labels, a change in their thinking regarding themselves must happen before new descriptions can be formed.

I Can't Write

Julie, a seventh-grader in my English class, was convinced that she would *never* be able to write a story. To Julie, filling up a page of writing was as insurmountable as Mt. Everest. Whenever Julie and I conferenced about her work, she would always comment, "I can't write," or, "I'm not a writer," at least once. One day, however, as I was walking past her desk, I noticed Julie finishing the back of a sheet of paper with quick strokes of her pencil. Both sides were full of her writing. About the same time, Julie noticed me and quickly hid the paper.

Educator: Wow, Julie, you just wrote two pages, and I thought you said you couldn't write. How did you do that?

Julie looked shocked that I hadn't confiscated the note and caused a scene (as the other teachers in our building would have). She turned to me:

Julie: I needed to tell Steffie what happened after school yesterday.

Educator: So, you just wrote a story for Steffie about what happened yesterday. And you thought you couldn't write stories. I'm impressed. (labelizing)

I left this question for Julie to consider on her own. The solutioning conversation was over. During our next writing conference, Julie shared that now that she knew she could write, she did. Her romance story was not the best I've ever read, but it was three pages long—three pages of personal learning material for grammar, punctuation, and spelling. In those three pages, Julie proved to herself that she could do something to which her mind had previously been closed. Julie beamed as she turned in her final draft. I was also overjoyed at not having to try convincing her of her abilities or to find ways to stimulate writing assignments in hopes that she would take the bait. Julie had discovered and described (labelized) herself (with just a little help from the language of solutioning) as a writer, and so she was.

Students of all ages can be so cruel to each other, from the classic bullies to the constant name-calling. It remains a mystery how some students overcome the names or labels their peers impose but others are devastated. Is it a matter of self-esteem, coping skills, or something else? Helping students handle teasing is a need for every educator. From the name-calling of elementary school (e.g., *stupid, sissy, crybaby, tattletale*) to the harshness of middle school (e.g., *fag, player, retard, dirty*) to the damaging reputations of high school (*e.g., stoner, druggie, whore, pregnant*), teasing and name-calling are powerful weapons students use against each other and can even result in physical violence. Frequently, the labels have some elements of truth. Sometimes issues of race, personal hygiene, behavior choices, and so on can be addressed when students are being teased, called names, or labeled. Use this opportunity to help students find solutions to problems that are encouraging, bringing on, or sustaining teasing. Most students are frustrated when told to "just ignore them and they'll stop." Solutioning will prepare you for when the next student comes into class crying, upset, mad, hurt, or just preoccupied by the labels of her or his peers. Begin a more hopeful view by labelizing (which may be all that is necessary).

List some labels, helpful or not, that some of your students carry around. Now try saying the same thing in language that sounds less permanent or serious. Or use MASTER 12 "Student Worksheet: Labelize" to get your students thinking with a solutioning focus. This can be done when the need arises during a problem situation or in advance as a whole-class activity/lesson.

MASTER 12

Confront the negative labels that students are carrying around with them to open the door for new thinking, changing, and solutioning.

What words/labels do you use to describe yourself?

I am _____.

What words/labels do others use when teasing or calling names?

They call me _____.

What is a more positive/accurate description?

_____

_____

What is a nicer, less harsh way to describe any hurtful labels or problems?

_____

_____

Does anything happen all of the time? Could you add *sometimes* to the label or description?

_____

_____

Are some parts of the label/description useful or are there some places/some times when it would be considered good?

_____

_____

Whenever you hear others or yourself say something critical, STOP and ask yourself, "What is another way I could describe that?"

_____

_____

Temporize

Just as the words we use to describe students and student problems may keep students in a prisonlike pattern, they can also be used to set students free. By attaching the word *sometimes* to problem descriptions, the doorway of opportunities is opened and a **purpose** can be created (Webb, 1999). The use of this word illustrates the solutioning focus that problems are not occurring 100% of the time (Metcalf, 1995). By discussing problems as only happening some of the time, you are illustrating that there are times when the problem does not happen and leading the way to an exploration of exceptions as **potential** solutions. Students, their parents, or both may feel better able to find solutions for *energetic sometimes* rather than *hyperactive*. Teachers can deal with *forgetful sometimes* with a more positive approach than *lazy*. The problems are the same, but the words help them seem less than all-encompassing and more temporary.

"Use of verbs like *show, become, seem* and *act as if* promote a view that behaviors are temporary and changeable" (Walter & Peller, 1992, p. 17). Saying that a student is acting sad or depressed has a very different connotation than saying the student *is* depressed. This is not to discount the seriousness of the problem, but to approach it in a way that provides hope. If we are to say that a student is rebellious sometimes, it is a very different outlook. We are all rebellious sometimes. "The presupposition is that she or he is acting that way now, but could be acting in other ways at other times" (Walter & Peller, 1992, p. 17). This paves the way to explore the exceptional times as clues to solutions.

In addition is the power in the little three-letter word *yet*. Attaching this word on the end of problem descriptions gives the idea that the problem is temporary and the solution will happen at some point in the future (Webb, 1999). For example, "Not passing yet" is much more encouraging than "failing." A **purpose** is more easily created and achieved.

According to the solutioning focus, problems are solvable. To express this idea, we must refer to them in the past. By using the past tense—*were* or *have/had been* versus *are*—we communicate to students our assumption that a solution will happen, the problem will get better, and they can do it. "You were behind" instead of "You are behind" creates an opportunity for growth and change, rather than a hopeless fact. This one change made a difference for a student named Murray, as sent in by a workshop participant who chose this one suggestion to take home to his classroom.

Tough Guy?

Sent in by a workshop participant

Murray, one of my fourth-grade students, was the tough guy. He had been in several fights. One day, he and another student began having words in the back of the classroom but seemed to work it out before I got there. After class, Murray and I got the chance to talk because he missed his bus. I decided to use the opportunity to put his idea of being a fighter in the past. I commented, "Murray, you have been a fighter in the past, but now that you are working things out, you won't be in the office anymore. That is pretty cool." He looked at me with a new look as he seemed to process what I had said. Then he kind of nodded and went back to his game. Later that week, I was on playground duty and saw all the kids running over to the swings, yelling, "Fight!" I got there just in time to hear Murray saying to the other student, "I used to be a fighter, but now I'm not. I don't want my mom called again. Just get lost." The other student looked a little surprised, gave Murray the swing, and walked away. I gave Murray a high five, and the bell rang.

Finally, temporize by creating an expectancy for the solution by using the word *when.* "When you are passing" or "When you catch up" shows the student that you automatically assume this will happen. Remember, we often live up to the expectations others have for us. Why not use this reality to put the solution in the future? Don't create room for failure with "If you catch up." Replace if with *when* in all references to expectations and solutions, and the results will follow.

Script for Success

Sent in by Mary Mills, eighth-grade language arts teacher, counselor (Used with permission from Mary Mills)

I was having writing conferences with all of my eighth-grade students on a weekly basis as part of our writer's workshop. The first place I decided to try the language of solutioning was during these conferences. I thought it would be a good experiment. While listening to the language suggestions, I realized that I summarized each conference with an "if"-type statement—for example, "If you fix the capitalization and add a conclusion, this will be great" and "If you type this, it'll be an A for sure." Many times, I was disappointed, however, because the changes/suggestions never happened. I decided to change to *when* and see whether it made a difference. I forced myself to say, "When you fix the capitalization, type, add a conclusion" and so on. When the stories came in, I couldn't believe it. Most of the changes/suggestions had been made. The grades were higher, and I felt as if the conferencing time had really paid off for once. By giving the assumption that the follow-through would happen with *when,* rather than creating doubt with *if,* it did. Language sure is a powerful tool.

Attention to detail may seem extreme, but the positive results are equally extreme. By training yourself to use the language of solutioning with students (see Chart 2.5 in MASTER 13 "Language Lesson: Temporize"), you will have incredible experiences.

Temporize

MASTER 13

Chart 2.5

Avoid permanent-sounding terms.	Use *sometimes* to make problems less permanent and to open the doorway for exceptions to be explored.
"I am always so dumb."	"Sometimes you feel dumb."
	Use *yet* to make the solution seem an inevitable part of the future.
"I am failing."	"You are not passing yet."
Avoid "being" verbs. "Tom is depressed."	Use "as if"-type verbs. "Tom acts as if he is depressed."
Avoid present tense verbs.	Use past tense verbs when referring to problems.
"You are tardy."	"You were tardy."
Get rid of *if.*	Show your assumption that students will find solutions with *when.*
"If you get all of your work in . . ."	"When you get all of your work in . . ."

SOURCE: Adapted from *Solutioning: Solution-Focused Interventions for Counselors* (pp. 70-71), by W. Webb, 1999, Philadelphia: Taylor and Francis/Accelerated Development. Used with permission.

Add your own here:

LANGUAGE LESSON

Normalize

Students not only feel as if they are problems, but sometimes they feel as if they are the only ones with problems. Most students have a desire, conscious or not, to be like all of the other students. Why do you think companies like Nike and Calvin Klein are multibillion-dollar entities? It doesn't take much for students to feel abnormal: a large nose, a different family constellation, K-Mart shoes, the wrong grades (too high or too low), and on and on. Descriptions that illustrate the commonness and the normalcy of the situation can lessen its power, lift the burden, and motivate a **purpose.** "Normalize—Speak about the concern as if it is in the realm of normal human experience, rather than an exotic or terrible thing" (O'Hanlon & Beadle, 1994, p. 40).

Share with students that you have dealt with "forgetfulness," "energetic students," "students who were sad sometimes," and so on before and that most people are forgetful or energetic or sad at times. Go back and look at your solutioning descriptions (labelizing). Could you add a phrase or sentence that makes the problem seem more normal? Sometimes that is all it takes, as illustrated in a telephone conversation I had with a parent.

Crazy or a Freshman

Adapted from *Solutioning: Solution-Focused Interventions for Counselors* (pp. 73-74), by W. Webb, 1999, Philadelphia: Taylor and Francis/Accelerated Development. Used with permission.

Linda, a worried mother, called me about getting her 14-year-old daughter into counseling. Linda described her daughter's many typical adolescent behaviors: limit testing, experimenting with various clothing styles, questioning the family chore divisions, and so on. Linda had concluded that her daughter was headed for some worst case scenario (e.g., rebellion, pregnancy, jail). She said she was nearly hopeless and a failure as a parent. Linda was sure her daughter's behavior indicated hatred. I shared with the mother that I work primarily with children of this age and that testing limits, questioning chores, and trying some trendy styles are common behaviors, especially of freshmen. The time when children enter high school and try really hard to grow up is typically a stressful one for many families, and most live through it and come out OK. She said, "Really, you mean these things are normal for some freshmen? Other families you know about go through this?" to which I replied that many children go through this stage. The mother's relief was amazing: "If this is a stage, then she probably doesn't hate me. You know, I think she does love me. And if this is a stage, then she's not going crazy or anything. We can handle this, we've been through stages before." I said I was sure they could.

Chapter 2 Focused   As you develop your solutioning focus, the tools for manipulating problems and establishing a joint **purpose** will be adapted into your personal script. When problems are externalized and described in ways that emphasize their temporary and common qualities, both you and your students will feel a sense of relief, a sense that is hopeful and motivating. When the view of problems begins to change, blaming and excuses end, and possible solutions fill the horizon. With a few statements and questions from this chapter, a joint **purpose** will be developed, and the focus will cease being the problem and become solutions instead.

Some students, however, may need to explore when the problem has not existed or has been better or to visualize a desired tomorrow before they gain enough hope to set a **purpose** for change. Be flexible. Rather than force a **purpose** on students, move into the **potentials** questions of the next chapter and the **purpose** will become a given.

3

Journey Through Solutioning
Potentials

*Potentials are solution options codiscovered with
students through an organized exploration.*

Finding Potentials

*With some students, hope is the hardest place to begin,
so the language of solutioning has it built in.*

As soon as students feel heard and have discussed a **purpose** for solutioning, an exploration of **potentials,** the heart of solutioning, can begin (see the Journey Through Solutioning Map in Figure 3.1)! During this step, students discover solutions they are capable of using and are propelled directly into a **plan.** Solutioning empowers students by providing four areas to find, visualize, or borrow **potential** solutions. **Potentials** are solution options codiscovered with students through an organized exploration that begins with skills, abilities, and exceptions that students already have and proceeds, if necessary, to skills, abilities, and ideas that are desired, visualized, or borrowed (Webb, 1998).

The first option is finding problem exceptions (*past potentials* and *present potentials*), helping students realize times before/without the problem. This is so encouraging that students who are resistive or hesitant regarding their **purpose** even become excited. The exceptions usually suggest easily applied solutions. Another option is discussing how things could be without the problem (*pretend potential*), moving students toward **plans** by building the solution vision and method to overcome problems and thus the desire and motivation to do so. A final option is borrowing solutions that have worked for other students or role models and/or enlisting support (*people potentials*), thus building hope and responsibility.

Many workshop and class participants adopt the language from this chapter first and then fill in the edges with the other Ps of the process. Notice

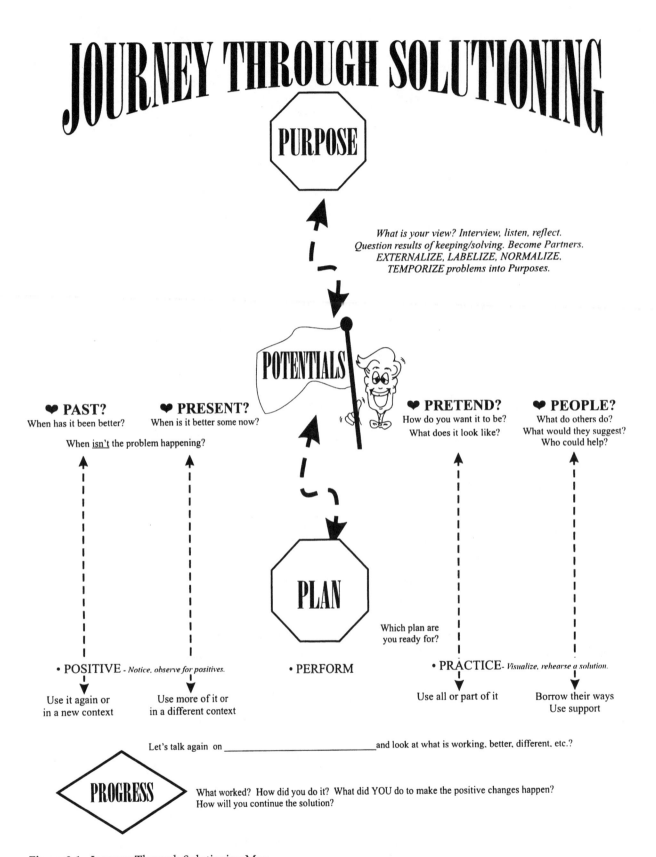

Figure 3.1. Journey Through Solutioning Map.

Willyn H. Webb, *The Educator's Guide to Solutioning.* Copyright © 1999 by Corwin Press, Inc.

Chart 3.1   Solutions: Getting There

Problem-Focused, Traditional	*Solutioning-Focused*
Brainstorm solutions (out of thin air)	Explore four areas for ideas through structured questioning
List/generate alternatives	"When isn't the problem happening?"
Tell students the solutions	"Pretend how you want things to be."
Give answers	"How might others solve this?"
Correct, reprimand	Lead, support
Lecture	Question

how the solutioning techniques and sample **potential** questions in Chart 3.1 enable students to find solutions.

Exceptional Potential

Solutioning allows students to find their own solutions by discovering times other than the problem. In our weight-conscious society, you'll readily understand the terms *low problem, nonproblem,* and *problem free*. Problems, negative behaviors, and poor skills do not happen all of the time (even though it may seem so). A problem may still exist but is less intense. In solution-focused brief therapy, these times are referred to as "exceptions" (de Shazer, 1985; de Shazer et al., 1986; Metcalf, 1995; O'Hanlon & Beadle, 1994; O'Hanlon & Weiner-Davis, 1989; Walter & Peller, 1992). This comes from the old adage that for every rule (which is the problem, in this case) there is an exception (time without or less of the problem). The exceptional times can be searched for solution ideas. "It has been our observation that regardless of the magnitude or chronicity of the problems people experience, there are situations or times when, for some reason, the problem simply does not happen" (O'Hanlon & Weiner-Davis, 1989, p. 82).

Are problem-free times ever considered by educators when discussing student problems? Rarely, it seems, and only in confusion as we sit around and beat our heads against the wall, trying to figure out why students act the way they do. Our most sincere and caring efforts for understanding rarely provide the solutions students need. All of the insight in the world does not give automatic ideas for change. Considering the low problem, nonproblem, or problem-free times, however, does open **potential** solutions. "[T]he exceptions to the problem offer a tremendous amount of information about what is needed to solve the problem. Solutions can be unearthed by examining the differences between times when the problem has occurred and times when it has not" (O'Hanlon & Weiner-Davis, 1989, p. 82).

Useful solution **potentials** or exceptions are those that have already happened in the past or are currently happening in the present. These **potentials** prove that students already have the abilities necessary to solve problems.

Anyone with any learning theory background knows the motivational repercussions of building on a previously learned skill. This is the idea of success breeding success applied to problem intervention. O'Hanlon and Weiner-Davis (1989) agree that, often, anyone with a problem simply needs to do more of what is already working until the problem no longer exists. We all know of "problem" students who behave properly or have success in some classes, with some peers, or on some days. Examining these times provides doable solutions.

In the past, I tended to dwell too much on the problem and let the student talk too much. I like this new approach so much. It saves so much time and energy. (Helena Burch, secondary Spanish teacher; used with permission from Helena Burch)

Students are often shocked when you ask about the nonproblem times instead of the usual lecturing on the evils of the problem or how things should be. Shock soon turns to relief and excitement. Most students can recall many instances of success and are eager to get a chance to share them. This leads right into solutions and **plans.**

Sometimes, however, students honestly cannot think about the exceptional times because they feel overwhelmed by the problem times. Through the continued use of questioning, students begin to see that the problem is not all-encompassing, and they begin to brighten, see light at the end of the tunnel, and come up with solutions to try. The questions assume that there are times when the problem occurs less or not at all. They encourage the sharing of happy, successful times. Who wouldn't enjoy this type of sharing, as opposed to lectures and reprimands? "The concept is so simple. If people want to experience more success, more happiness, and less stress in their lives, help them assess what is different about the times when they are already successful, happy and stress-free" (O'Hanlon & Weiner-Davis, 1989, p. 83)

Boredom Buster: Coming to Class Prepared

Curtis sauntered into class, nothing in his hands, as carefree as could be. This was the third day in a row that he had forgotten to bring materials to class. This highly intelligent student was becoming more frustrating to me by the minute. How could he ever pass my class if he never did any work? I was torn between trying to teach responsibility by allowing him to suffer the consequences of a failing grade OR helping him learn by having pencils, papers, and extra books available in the room for checkout. I tried solutioning instead:

Educator: Curtis, what is different about days when you bring your stuff to class? (problem exception-*present potential* question)

Curtis: Oh, that's easy, I just tell myself to.

The simplicity of his answer almost made me laugh. I knew we had an exception and must build on it.

Educator: Wow, that's a skill. How do you do that, remember to tell yourself to bring them?

His answer took a little longer this time.

Curtis: I guess I just think about how bored I am when I do nothing in class, and that reminds me. (clarifying **potential** question)

I felt as if we were getting somewhere.

Educator: So, when you don't want to be bored, you remember your stuff. What do you think would help remind you of boredom so that you'd tell yourself to bring your stuff more often? (restate **potential, plan**)

We were moving from the **potentials** to the **plan.** I felt as if he needed to use what works for him sometimes all of the time.

Curtis: Hey, I have this cool bumper sticker that says Boredom Sucks. Do you think I could put it in my locker so I'd remember when I see it and tell myself to get my book?

This **plan** was completely his, and he seemed motivated that it would work. Although I was not too pleased with the language of the bumper sticker, I thought that, in sticking with my solutioning focus, I needed to let him try his solution. Curtis brought the bumper sticker for his locker and his materials to class almost every day for the rest of the semester. He passed my class, and I didn't have to make any deep, inner decisions about forcing responsibility or enabling students. I simply gave Curtis the respect and opportunity to find his own exceptions and to build on them for his solution.

I didn't think Curtis cared enough to come prepared. I had been brainstorming ways to motivate him to learn. It turned out that he needed to do it himself. Not doing anything was boring for him. I had thought he enjoyed doing nothing and tried to get away with it. Where I saw no **potential** solutions, Curtis found a simple one.

With some students, hope is the hardest place to begin, so the language of solutioning has it built in. Not all interactions go so smoothly. Even when the exceptions found do not lead directly to an acceptable **plan,** the partnership has been formed, and continued questions/exploration allow solutions to emerge that work for students and educators.

Do You Hear What I Hear?

As your solutioning focus develops, your listening skills will be fine-tuned. Amid complaining, blaming, and whining, you will hear exceptions and **potentials.** With one little question, you will change the direction of the conversation and find positives you never imagined were there. Often, students don't even realize what they have said and are pleasantly surprised to learn of the exceptions to their problems and **potential** solutions. As you begin hearing more of the exceptions, the positives, and the **potentials,** you can then point it out, accentuate it, and give it to students to use for their own solutions. Contrast this with telling them what to do, giving advice, or reprimanding. You are getting from and giving back to students their own solutions.

Remember to give enough wait time! Effective responses after you hear something useful is, "Say that again . . . Do you realize what you just said?" This questioning allows students to discover for themselves the value in their words. As you continue your solutioning journey, make it a habit to begin practicing solutioning-focused listening, almost tuning out problem talk and searching for minute exceptions and glimmers of **potential.** You will be amazed at what you find.

I have noticed that our time together has been much more productive because we are not wasting so much time on the problem. (Sandi Kropuenske, high school science teacher)

Proactive Potential

It may be helpful for your own solutioning focus to take a minute, especially when facing a difficult situation or a stubborn student, to look at the exceptions/solution possibilities you see in the student/situation *before* the solutioning conversation. By doing your homework, so to speak, you will have a more hopeful outlook, which will come across with students in your assumptions/persistence in questioning. The questions on MASTER 14 "Educator Helpsheet: Proactive Potential" will take you through the process for finding **potentials.** This sheet is designed for you to do alone. Specific worksheets and questions to use with students follow later, after each section of **potential** solutions. You may also want to ask the questions of yourself. We all need a little motivation at times, especially with those difficult students who come along every so often. Do not think that each solutioning conversation requires this much preparation or planning. Most of the time, they just happen.

MASTER 14

Get ready for tough students by building up a reservoir of **potentials.** In trying situations, this exercise may give you the boost, the hope, and the motivation you need to lead students toward their own solution **potentials.**

POTENTIAL from the *PAST*

When or where has the student NOT had the problem? (You may need to do some research here. Ask past teachers, parents, etc.)

_____

_____

_____

What is different about the times when the student is doing the solution (not doing the problem)?

_____

_____

_____

How have you (or the student) overcome the problem before? What did you (or the student) do that was different/better?

_____

_____

_____

What has the student (or you) said/done/thought/felt better in the past?

_____

_____

_____

(continued)

MASTER 14 Continued

PRESENT POTENTIAL

When doesn't the problem bother you or the student?

_____

_____

_____

What part of the day is better for you (or the student)? Why?

_____

_____

_____

What works (even a little) against the problem now? By you? By the student?

_____

_____

_____

How are you coping? How is the student coping?

_____

_____

_____

What do you do that works? What does the student do that works?

_____

_____

_____

What current skills does the student have?

_____

_____

_____

MASTER 14 Continued

PRETEND POTENTIAL

How do you want things to be for you? For the student? Describe it.

_____

_____

_____

What could you (or the student) be doing instead or differently?

_____

_____

_____

Pretend the problem is not a problem (is fixed). What happens?

_____

_____

_____

PEOPLE POTENTIAL

Who currently helps you:?

_____

_____

_____

What helps others? Could a solution be borrowed?

_____

_____

_____

Name the positive people in the student's life.

_____

_____

_____

(continued)

MASTER 14 Continued

Who has made an impact or had influence on the student in the past? Could you recruit him/her/them now?

_____

_____

_____

Does the student have a good support system in place? Could you help the student form one?

_____

_____

_____

Summarize your list here:

Solution **potentials** I have: Solution **potentials** the student has:

_____   _____

_____   _____

_____   _____

_____   _____

_____   _____

_____   _____

_____   _____

_____   _____

_____   _____

_____   _____

_____   _____

_____   _____

Use the back of this sheet if necessary.

Most students have had times before the problem (even if you have to go way back); remember when things were better, when they were successful, when things were different; and are anxious to share them. Hints for solutions will be discovered. Once students believe that they have had a chance to vent and feel heard and understood, it is important to move them toward this type of positive exploration.

With some students, those times may be difficult to recall. In fact, when the whole idea of times without or before the problem comes up, you may get blank stares. Blank stares of trying to remember positive times is a better activity than continued blaming, numerous excuses, or wallowing in self-pity. O'Hanlon and Weiner-Davis (1989) share the typical reaction they get: "They often are quiet momentarily and appear to be lost in thought. The reason for this silence is that people generally cast the events in their lives in black and white terms" (p. 83). We all do this, but children and adolescents are especially susceptible to black-and-white thinking. No one is always late, always sad, always failing everything, or always in trouble. Situations are perceived, however, in an all-or-nothing way. A change in this perception takes a change in thinking. Using questioning, exploring, and sharing of your perceptions helps expand students' views, and the students will begin seeing some light in their problem tunnel. These tunnels often become fully lit when the students realize there are times when they control the problem, or the problem is better, or they remember a time without the problem. Metcalf (1995) discusses the value of reminiscing, calling it "a natural tranquilizer":

> What does reminiscing do for us? It often changes our perception of life events, people, experiences, and even future events. It reminds us that there have been happier times. Most of all, it changes our focus from one of problem saturation to that of a time when problems seemed less dominant . . . When working with students, teachers, parents, and administrators, searching for more efficient, successful, happier times solicits solutions. (p. 9)

If nothing else is accomplished through a discussion of past experiences without the problem, the mood becomes more conducive to further exploration. The recollection of past positives is a safe place, one where students can remove themselves from the current (problem) situation. It motivates students toward establishing a **purpose** of not having the problem in their lives anymore. As you begin to question about past times without the problem and get the blank stares and the "I don't knows," remember that students may be "problem saturated" (White & Epston, 1990). It may take time, creative strategies, many ways of asking the same question, and even your own observations to help students uncover the problem-free times as a means toward solutions that they are already capable of achieving.

**Past Potential:
Let History
Repeat Itself**

For those who tend to be stuck in the past, who tend to blame it or use it as an excuse, looking at *past potential* allows you to acknowledge their point of view, but assist them in using the past positively. Cathy Crane, a principal, used these ideas with a teacher who could not get out of her past full of excuses in the following evaluation conference.

Do It Again

Journal entry of Cathy Crane, principal (Used with permission from Cathy Crane)

I had to stop her from talking and making excuses for just a minute. I asked her to stop and think about her past lessons. Then I asked her which ones she thought were the most successful. We talked about what she thought had made them successful. I told her that was what I wanted her to think about when she wrote her next lesson plans.

The next example shows how quickly a solution can be discovered. I added parenthetical explanations to highlight Nancy's brilliant use of solutioning.

Never Say Never

Journal entry of Nancy Kienapfel, K-12 counselor (Used with permission from Nancy Kienapfel)

One of the elementary teachers asked me to talk with one of her students who was having a hard time at recess. Apparently, he thinks that no one wants to play with him. According to the teacher, when she asks others to group with him or play with him, they willingly do so and she has not noticed anyone teasing him or harassing him. I asked Carlos to tell me about the times when he thought the other students liked to play with him. (exception–*past potential* question)

Carlos: Never.

Me: How about when you were in kindergarten? (feeding the *past potential,* reasking the question)

Carlos: They played with me then. (exception/**potentials** statement)

Me: How did you get the kids to play with you last year? (clarify, define **potentials**)

Carlos: I asked them. (**potential** solution statement)

Me: Do you ask the other kids if you can play with them now? (bring **potentials** into present)

Carlos: No.

Me: Do you think that would work now?

Carlos: Maybe.

Me: Would you try it and let me know how it works? (**plan**)

Carlos: Sure.

   The next day, after recess, I saw Carlos in the hall and asked him how recess was, and he smiled and said, "OK!"

   MASTER 15 "Language Lesson: Past Potential" gives many questioning suggestions for helping students find solution **potentials** from the past, their own lost treasure. These have been adapted from O'Hanlon and Weiner-Davis (1989), Metcalf (1995), and Walter and Peller (1992). You may want to practice these with a role-play partner before trying them with students, just to hear yourself and see the reactions, or use the sheet during solutioning as a reminder.

Past Potential

MASTER 15

What is different about times when _____ (e.g., you do the assignment, you are on time, you get along)? This assumes those times DO exist.

Have there been times when you were able to talk to a teacher in a calm way? How did you do it? How would the teacher say you did it?

In the past, when you have (positive description), what were you *doing*? What were you *thinking*? What were you *saying*?

How did your day go differently when you did not have the problem?

When was the last time you were happy/successful/comfortable in school? What were you doing then that was different/better/worked? How?

How have you overcome/controlled the problem before? What did you do that was different/better?

How have you _____ (e.g., avoided problems, done assignments, made friends) in the past? What has worked before?

What are some things you do that help when _____ (e.g., you're bored, confused, mad)?

You've coped/lived with this problem this long. Cool. How have you done it?

You have been in school for _____ years now, and you've made it! How?

Tell me about times when things were better, different, more of what you want.

How did you get _____ (e.g., get the fight to stop, her to be your friend again, the kids off your back, your homework done)?

What do you do for fun? When are you happy, relaxed, OK?

LANGUAGE LESSON

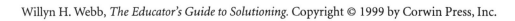

Past Potential

MASTER 15 Continued

Have you ever had this problem in the past? How did you deal with it/fix it/resolve it then? What would you need to do to get that to happen again?

Perhaps you can get to know the student and the other areas of his or her life. Many ideas can come from places or situations where the problem doesn't intrude. "Reminisce."

Remember, we are hunting for lost treasure, and many clues are necessary. It is rare that the chest is found full of gold. Sometimes many hints toward abilities, any small successes, or glimmers of hope have to be used and the solution constructed from there.

SOURCE: Adapted from *Solutioning: Solution-Focused Interventions for Counselors* (pp. 90-91), by W. Webb, 1999, Philadelphia: Taylor and Francis/Accelerated Development. Used with permission.

Add your own here:

LANGUAGE LESSON

Present Potential: There Is No Better Time

Finding and building on **potentials** for solutions that are already happening in students' lives is the most motivating exploration (Webb, 1999). When students know they have the ability and just need to do more of it, they feel capable and confident. *Present potential* is the most rapid route to take in solution construction. We all know that children live in the moment. Their reality is now, and solutioning uses it for all it is worth. Keeping the conversation in the present and future also prevents any opportunities to use the past as an excuse or to find places for blame.

Finding exceptions to problems and **potential** solutions within the present, however, can also be the most difficult. Some students feel completely encompassed by their problem in their present reality; thus, it is very difficult for them to see the gray areas or times when the problem does not exist. Questioning with understanding and empathy is our tool in helping students find the exceptions and, in the process, a new and more hopeful outlook on their present problem situation.

Oh, Henry

As shared by a workshop participant

So far this semester, a freshman named Henry had been in trouble in my class for throwing spitballs, talking loudly during instruction, and cussing at another student. He was not a bad kid, just overly adolescent. The day I tried solutioning, Henry had not done any of the assignment (on some days he did, so I knew he had **potential**) and had tried to socialize the entire period. I looked over my solutioning notes and then asked, "Henry, what are you doing differently when you do complete assignments?" In his smarty freshman sort of way, Henry replied, "I just don't talk and do it." He had just given me the answer I had wanted to give him. I couldn't believe it. We were short on time, so I merely responded, "Oh, so when you don't talk, you complete the assignment. Good to know you're on top of it." He gave me a weird look because I hadn't done the typical when-you-come-to-class-tomorrow-don't-talk-and-do-the assignment-or-your-grade-will-be-a-D type of lecture. I left it at that, and for the next 3 days, Henry didn't talk (or throw spitballs or cuss) but did complete assignments.

I really believe that my question had helped him realize his own *present potential* that he could do the work, when he chose to, when he didn't talk so much. He made the right choice most of the time from then on and ended up with a B in my class. Thanks to solutioning.

MASTER 16 "Language Lesson: Present Potential" gives sample questions to try in helping students realize their own abilities at dealing with, coping with, or overcoming the problem each day.

Present Potential

MASTER 16

How does your day go when (the exception happens/the problem doesn't)?

When during the day is the problem less/better? What are you doing/thinking differently then?

When are you already doing some of _____ (e.g., your homework, being on time, walking away from fights, any goal or problem opposite)?

When isn't this problem happening? What is it different?

What is going good in your life right now?

When are you enjoying school/class?

What do you like about each day? Can you describe it?

What are you doing differently when you are completing part of the assignment (or other positive behavior)?

SOURCE: Adapted from the work of de Shazer, 1988; Metcalf, 1995; O'Hanlon & Weiner-Davis, 1989; and Walter & Peller, 1992, as used in Webb, 1999.

Add your own here:

LANGUAGE LESSON

Chart 3.2 Observations

Problem-Focused, Traditional	Solutioning-Focused
"Sit down."	"I just realized you have been in your seat(s) all morning. How did you do that?"
"Be quiet."	"You are listening so well. How are you doing it?"
"Get to work."	"You have completed 10 minutes of work. I'm impressed."
"You're late."	"You're on time. Now tell me how you did it."
"I've had it."	"This has been a great afternoon."
"Shape up or else."	"You did this spelling test without looking around. What was different?"

Observe What Works

Getting in the habit of positive observation is actualizing the solutioning focus.

A favorite solutioning technique of many is observing what works—noticing when students are doing things right, using a solution, or not having the problem. This is a form of helping students realize and use their *present potentials* for solving problems. By getting in the habit of noting and sharing with students when you see things working, you form a knowledge base for solutions. These may be used as past exceptions and **potentials** at some point in the future or in the moment to illustrate for students their current abilities, competencies, and solutions.

The timing and language used are crucial. For the most effective use of the situation, use the student's name, mention the behavior clearly, and then end with a curiosity-based question (Metcalf, 1995). For example, you notice that John, a typical third-grade ADHD student, has stayed in his place during the entire story today and say, "John, you haven't let energy get you out of your seat all morning. How did you do that?" By following these guidelines, students remain in possession of their own solution and are made experts of their ability, and motivation for continuing the behavior becomes intrinsic. Notice the difference, shown in Chart 3.2.

Really knowing your students comes in handy here. For some teachers, this may be embarrassing, doing more damage to their cause than helping it. If this is the case, a note, a private moment in the hall, or sharing with parents may be helpful in getting across the message that the student does have and sometimes uses solutions.

Observing what works is a learned skill, and the more you can train yourself and teach your students to do it, the more you will see. Sometimes just noticing is all it takes for the solution actually to become the solution.

Wow!

Journal entry of Romagean Personne, K-12 art teacher (Used with permission from Romagean Personne)

This was the case for one of my first adult students with her two case studies, high school boys on the verge of dropping out to pursue careers as drug dealers. Mrs. Personne thought that small steps toward success would be more effective with the boys than taking on the task of selling them on graduating. The following is a page from Mrs. Personne's journal.

Thursday, October 24, 1996

Well, what do you know! Wow! Both boys were on time to school this morning and made it to all of their classes on time. When they came into mine, I acted surprised and said, "Wow, Sam and Lou, how did you do it?"

Sam: Do what, Mrs. Personne?

Me: Get to school on time this morning and to my class before the bell.

Friday, October 25, 1996

Sam was on time to school and even showed up early. Lou was not tardy either. When I walked into my room after lunch, I found both boys waiting for me. I quickly looked at the clock and noticed that we still had 5 minutes left.

Me: Wow, Lou and Sam, just look at you! Did you know that you are 5 minutes early? How did you do that?

Lou: It is cold outside, and we were freezing.

Me: Hey, maybe it will be cold more days.

Sam: Mrs. Personne, you really do not mean that.

I didn't get to respond right then.

Monday, October 28, 1996

Both boys came to my class on time, a little early again.

Me: Hey, Lou and Sam, I see you are early to class! It's not cold outside today. How did you do it?

Sam: I guess, Mrs. Personne, we just cannot be late anymore 'cause you keep noticing when we're not.

Mrs. Personne was extremely good at noticing when things were going right and helping her students notice too. She did so in a way that did not make her the authority or expert, but that allowed the students to realize and own their own successes, accomplishments, and **potentials.** Her language, which was scripted from solutioning, was the key. Mrs. Personne shared that it felt awkward at first, but she forced herself to just say it. The results were so wonderful that she couldn't wait to say it again. Observing what works, works!

Al Williams, a master teacher and principal of many years, commented to a female student, "I like your handling of that tardy stuff" when she finally came in on time one day, and he did not have to deal with it again. Not only is observing what works an effective intervention with students, but it is also a burnout preventer for teachers. The power of perspective cannot be under-sold. Getting in the positive observation habit is actualizing the solutioning focus. Al Williams concluded, "Observing for positives is really fun and equally as easy as looking for negatives. I plan to do much more of this" (quotes used by permission from Al Williams).

MASTER 17 "Language Lesson: Observe What Works" gives guidelines for observing what works and using the **potentials** of the present.

Observe What Works

MASTER 17

1. Pick an appropriate time and place to share your observation.
2. Use the most effective means of relaying the **potentials** you see. (verbal, written, other)
3. Use language that assumes change is or will be occurring.
4. Make the student the expert and use his or her name.
5. Mention clearly the problem that is being overcome OR the solution that is being used.
6. Use an exception-searching question so that the students can realize the internal **potentials** they are currently using.
7. End with a responsibility-giving question like "How did you do that?"

FOR EXAMPLE

Chad, I've just realized that you haven't let "anger" overpower you all morning and keep you out of your desk. How have you done that?

Wow, Austin, just look at you. Did you know that you've been on time to my class for 3 days in a row? How did you do that?

Dawn, you were so upset with your friends at lunch today that you got detention, yet you came to class and got to work. How have you calmed yourself down so fast? Does this happen a lot, that you calm down so well? How do you do that for yourself?

After class I noticed, Christine, that you turned in your assignment today. What is different about today, that you were able to use your class time, do the work, and turn it in before leaving? How exactly did you do it?

SOURCE: The language suggestions and examples are adapted and expanded from *Counseling Toward Solutions: A Practical Solution-Focused Program for Working With Students, Teachers, and Parents* by L. Metcalf, 1995, New York: Center for Applied Research in Education.

LANGUAGE LESSON

Willyn H. Webb, *The Educator's Guide to Solutioning.* Copyright © 1999 by Corwin Press, Inc.

Pretend Potential:
Use Your
Imagination

If you can get students to describe positive behavior, the
likelihood that it will happen increases tremendously.

If questioning for problem exceptions has not enlightened any solution ideas, another choice is *pretend*. This is a noncompulsive approach to solutions that enables you to read the "kid," not the problem. Simply ask, maybe even before the other **potentials** questions, "How do you want things to be?" or "Pretend this is better. What are you doing differently?" Questions like these give direction to the construction of solutions without putting students on the spot by asking for answers.

By discussing the desired, positive future, the blaming, excuses, and causes are all made obsolete. With just a few words, forward motion begins: *Pretend how you want it to be.* Students do not want to fail, get in trouble, or have difficulties in school. They want to succeed, be liked by the teacher, and get along with the other students. Admitting it and visualizing it are half the battle. By pretending a solution, students get to remove themselves from the constraints of the problem for a moment and to experience how it feels to be problem free. This feeling in itself can motivate them to begin taking some steps toward that solution immediately. By describing what it would look like and what they will be doing differently when the problem is better, students gain insight and ideas into the process necessary to achieve the solution. Walter and Peller (1992) have found that "introducing a conversation around a life without the problem allows people to enter the realm of possibility" (p. 77).

Granted, some of the pretend vision may be unrealistic, unattainable, or unlikely. Within, however, are always clues to solutions and small glimpses of positive behaviors that could be tried.

Movie-Making Marla

Marla, a seventh-grader, came into my counseling office after lunch. She was sobbing so hard that I could not understand a word she was saying. After a few more gasping sobs, she caught her breath enough to speak. "He hates me. My life is over. I never want to come to school again." First, I spent some time listening, reflecting feelings and meanings.

W.W.: You are very sad right now because you feel as if (as opposed to does) Matt hates you. It sounds as if you don't know whether you could come to school without him for a boyfriend.

Marla: He'll never go out with me again, and I don't know what to do.

W.W.: Could you tell me how you would like things to be? (Sounds like a dumb question, whose answer is obvious, but it puts her right into her solution description, as opposed to other questions for which the entire relationship might have been rehashed and no **plan** for the future formed.)

Marla: I'd like it if we liked each other. We'd call each other and go over to each other's houses.

W.W.: That sounds nice. What else?

Marla: We'd eat lunch together at the main table each day. We'd tell each other everything and never fight.

W.W.: What could *you* do to make it that way?

Marla: I don't know.

Of course, it is tempting here to start talking to her about hanging out with her girlfriends for a while. If I were to do this, it would make me the expert on what was best for her. I wanted to empower her, let her make her own decision and feel a sense of control over her life. My gut feeling is that different friends would not have been very appealing to Marla at that moment anyway. So focus and mouth control are important. Having a "script" or "map" is helpful.

W.W.: Marla, use your dream of how you want things to be and walk me through a day from the time you get on the bus.

Marla: I would get on the bus and smile and say hi to Brittany. I would go sit by her, and we would talk about our homework on the way to school. When we get off the bus, Brittany usually goes to the gym and I go talk to Matt. I walk up and say "hey," and we start talking. (She begins to sob.) But now he probably won't talk to me. In my dream, he talks to me.

W.W.: You're right. We can't control him, and he may or may not talk to you. It's cool the way you smile and say hi and start up conversations. I'm impressed. You sound like an outgoing person. Now, what are *you* doing in this picture that *you* could do tomorrow?

Marla: I could say hi and sit with Brittany. I guess I could try going over to Matt and see what he does.

W.W.: How does that feel, to think about going up to him tomorrow and saying "hey"?

Marla: It's scary, but I do it every morning, so I think I could.

During this conversation, Marla has gone from a victim who could never come to school again to an outgoing girl who could say, "Hey." After a little more practice with her **plan** and setting a time frame (at the end of the day tomorrow) to talk again, Marla went off empowered. The next morning, I happened to have bus duty and got to watch Marla create her movie in real life. She and Brittany got off the bus together. (By the way, in traditional interventions, Marla might have been encouraged to just hang out with Brittany instead. In this case, Marla never would have faced her fears and would have remained a victim of Matt.) However, if she would have chosen to go to the gym with Brittany, or any other solution, it would have been equally supported. As I watched Marla walk across the schoolyard toward Matt, I saw her take a deep breath, put on her smile, and say, "Hey." I noticed I was holding my breath, waiting for the reaction, so I reminded myself that the reaction was not important. Marla had tried her solution. To satisfy your curiosity, Matt did begin talking to her in what seemed a friendly way. During our follow-up discussion, we celebrated all of the skills Marla had and used to make her pretend solution a reality.

Students react in many ways when questioned about how a situation will look when it is better, different, or solved. Imagining a time without the problem, describing in detail what they might be doing, thinking, or feeling differently, however, is very much within all students' capabilities. The way *pretend* is introduced is important. Unless a heavy emphasis is placed on the *positive*, the personal, and the process (discussed further in Chapter 4), the discussion is merely a brainstorming session. The pioneers of solution-focused brief therapy at the Brief Family Therapy Center in Milwaukee use the "miracle question," which goes like this:

> Suppose that one night, while you were asleep, there was a miracle and this problem was solved. How would you know? What would be different? How will your husband know without your saying a word to him about it? (de Shazer, 1988, p. 5)

This is a very effective tool that you will want to adapt to fit your students by using language that will not seem silly. A version very effective with students, especially those who know everything and want total control of their lives, is this:

> *How do you want things to be?* followed with *What does it look like? Tell me what you are doing/thinking/saying/feeling differently when you come to school tomorrow and this is happening* (e.g., you are friends, you are passing math).

Describing *what it looks like* is the difficult part for students, but also the part that gives keys to solutions, things they can begin trying immediately (Webb, 1999). Sometimes it is helpful to feed them a little. It seems they have a picture in their minds but cannot describe it behaviorally (Webb, 1999). You may want to ask about details: Tomorrow when you walk in the door, what will you be doing differently? Will you say hi? Will you eat lunch together? Will you walk to class together? How did you do that? (Webb, 1999).

In another example,

> In your *pretend,* do you have your homework assignment? What are you doing with it? What do I (the teacher) say? What do you do next?

By asking for details of the pretend solution, you get answers like, "I'll just smile at her when I walk in" or "I'll put my homework in the basket." These are small-step behaviors that students can try tomorrow and be on the road to the solution. Most often, they are skills students already have but are not currently using. If you can get students to describe positive behavior, the likelihood that it will happen increases tremendously (Webb, 1999).

Many times, students want to change others first as a condition of their desired solution. When they are describing the other students not teasing them, their moms waking them up with breakfast in bed so that they are not tardy, and so on, the word *you* must be stressed in your questioning. This is an intervention of empowerment. Gently forcing students through questioning helps them create movies of their futures in which they control their fates. During their movies, you sometimes have to pause them and re-ask the questions, "What are *you* doing? What would so and so say *you* could do to make it that way?" This helps some students break away from victimhood and into responsibility and self-control.

Creating a Dream Team

During pretend, some indirect teaching is set up to happen. When a trusting, caring relationship exists between educator and student and a solutioning focus is ongoing, the responsibility given students is not diminished by educator input and sharing. Sometimes it is helpful to share your vision of what the student is doing and what it looks like when the problem no longer exists. This is a very different scenario from an educator telling a student how it's going to be. Although the same end is often created, the means make all the difference. Just ask whether the student would like to hear your pretend solution. The answer is almost always yes. Then share a very successful vision, one the student is capable of achieving. Tell it like a bedtime story in which the student is a character (regardless of the age). Smiles are abundant during the telling, and at the end the student usually has a few new ideas to try as **potential** solutions (Webb, 1999).

Once Upon a Time . . .

Journal entry of Delaine Hudson, sixth-grade teacher (Used with permission from Delaine Hudson)

Alex came in during recess crying. All of his friends, he said, hated him for some unclear reason. In reality, most of the children liked Alex. It was the three "popular" boys who were currently not speaking to him. After talking about times in the past when Alex had made friends, about when he had lived through them being mad before, and about the things he does to be a good friend, we had a lot of things that "worked" for Alex. However, he just couldn't visualize any of that making a difference for him right now. He didn't think he could face recess ending and the other children coming back in the room. So I asked him whether I could share my imagined movie about after recess. He agreed. I tried to emphasize the normalcy of the routine and the skills he had to handle the situation.

Once upon a time, the bell rings and I go and stand at the door. Alex begins getting out the math workbooks and putting one on each desk. As the other students come in, I greet them at the door and tell them to sit down and open to page 38. (Kevin is always the first one in.) Alex says, "Hi, Kevin," and smiles. Kevin says, "Hi," back. Then Alex says, "Hi," and smiles to each of the students as they pass each other. He asks Larry whether he won at four square and tells Lisa, "Page 38," when she asks. As Mike (the one who is mad at him) walks in, Alex says, "Hi, Mike." Then to each of the others. Then I interrupt the noise by going to the front of the room and beginning class. We talk about the problems on page 38 and then do a practice page.

At this time, the bell was really about to ring, so I stopped and asked Alex whether he could try to act out any small parts of my movie right now. He nodded. I asked him to get the math workbooks ready. The bell rang. Alex did greet many of these students and was smiling a lot. He didn't actually say "Hi" to Mike, but his demeanor was so normal that the fight blew over. By the end of the day, the boys were talking again (unfortunately, even when they should have been working). Alex just needed a **plan** for the unknown, a blueprint for action, which my imaginary movie provided. He already had the skills necessary; he just lacked the vision (provided by me) and the self-confidence (provided by the look at **potentials**).

You can introduce *pretend potential* solutions in many ways. Make it appropriate for the student and the situation. Some suggestions are found in MASTER 18 "Language Lesson: Pretend Potential." No matter a person's age, we all need to visualize a successful future in order to make it happen. You may want to use MASTER 18 "Language Lesson: Pretend Potential" almost like a script at first, with a partner or with students. In fact, you can use these questions in the form of an assignment, whether or not a problem even exists.

Pretend Potential

MASTER 18

Pretend how you want it (things) to be.

What will it look like when the problem is solved?

What is the first thing you do on a day without the problem.

Pretend everything is how you want it. Now describe what you are doing.

Imagine yourself using the solution. Describe what you are doing.

When you are on your way to fixing the problem, what are you doing?

If a miracle happened tonight and you woke up with the problem solved or were reasonably confident you were on a track to solving it, what would you be doing differently?

So, let's say tomorrow you wake up and you have not yet finished your homework but you are thinking you are on-track to getting it done. What are you doing differently?

After the problem is fixed . . . If I were a bug on the wall, what would I see you doing differently? How would others in your family know?

If we had a magic wand and it made _____ (e.g., boredom, anger, confusion, not caring) disappear, what would you be doing differently?

Let's visualize like athletes. You are _____ (e.g., getting along with your friends, finishing your assignments on time, understanding math). What are you doing? What does that look like?

Make up a movie of tomorrow without the problem. Tell it to me so that I'll feel as if I went to see it too.

SOURCE: Adapted from Webb, 1999; and Walter & Peller, 1992.

Add your own:

LANGUAGE LESSON

People Potential:
The Final Frontier

Students find the abilities or the ideas needed
to solve the problem within themselves.

Solutioning educators hope that students find the abilities, the ideas needed to solve the problem, within themselves. Students are just that, however, students or learners. In some cases, students may not have or be able to access the needed resources, skills, or abilities within their experience or imagination. Solutioning questions can still be used to give control and responsibility. First, you can explore with students how others might solve the problem and, second, how others might help them solve the problem. This approach teaches two skills: (a) how to draw from the positive modeling of others and (b) how to access and use human resources. With these two life skills under their belts, most students would be ready to take on the world. These two life skills, however, are rarely found in the curriculum.

How many students do you know who secretly wish they were like so and so, the smartest, cutest, toughest person in the school? How many students can you think of who wish they could handle problems as their dads or grandparents did in the old days? How many students strive to be more like big brother or the girl on television last night? Why not use these desires to help students draw on some *positive potential* behaviors that will lead to solutions?

Up, Up, and Away

Chris had more energy than necessary, couldn't sit still, was girl crazy (hitting or kicking them for interaction), and hated homework. Chris did have goals, however. He hadn't turned in an assignment all year but talked constantly about someday flying airplanes. (I'd tried making his assignments applicable to flight, with no avail.) When we talked about **potential** solutions to his failing grades, he couldn't come up with much. The truth was, he had never had very much success in school, was a victim of social promotion, couldn't do grade-level work even if he were to try, but had not quite qualified for special programs. Because Chris had never considered himself a student, he had trouble even imagining himself doing things differently.

Therefore, during our solutioning conversation, we ended up with *people potentials* as our last point of exploration. I asked Chris whom he admired most, and he answered with the name of some famous pilot. I asked Chris who in the school was most like that pilot. He named Ara, who was a good student and a nice boy. I continued and asked Chris what his pilot or Ara might do in Chris's situation. He said they would probably go in for help before school and do the homework at home, maybe even let Mom check it afterward. I agreed that people like the pilot and Ara usually do what they need to do to pass school, like getting help and doing homework. We discussed the details of what people like that do, and then I asked Chris whether he could pick one small part of it to try for a few days. He chose coming in for help before school. This started him on the road, and the last I heard he is in the Air Force as an airplane mechanic working toward flight lessons.

By stepping outside himself, whom he considered hopeless, and into the actions of others, Chris was able to experiment with some new behaviors. "Trying a little bit of what works for others is often a first step toward realizing one's own capabilities" (Webb, 1999, p. 110).

Finding and using role models or peers is a skill that can be enhanced by classroom activities. Metcalf (1995) shares an activity called "Positive People in Our Lives":

Use a wall and have students bring in a picture of a positive person, a parent, sibling, aunt, uncle, or neighbor. The person they choose should be someone they admire, who makes them smile and see the world differently—so differently that they feel good and "positive" when being around them. Discuss the following questions:

1. Whom do you know that is a positive person in your life?
2. What does the person do that makes him or her a positive person?
3. What does that person do that makes him or her seem positive to you?
4. How does knowing a positive person change your life?

The ultimate value in a project like this is when a problem does arrive. If a student is struggling with solution **potentials,** you simple ask, "How might your positive person handle this?" or "What advice would your positive person give you right now?" The picture and the resource are right there and available for the student to access.

Unfortunately, some students have a difficult time finding a truly positive person in their lives. For this reason, a hero story/project makes a fun assignment. This can easily be adapted to any grade level. Watch excerpts from hero movies (beyond the Superman types, including historical and current examples) and discuss the qualities of heroes. This makes an excellent inter-disciplinary unit—for example, list qualities, draw pictures, make comic books, fill out hero questionnaires, read history as prewriting activities. The cumulative project is a "My Hero" description or story, real or imagined. During this type of assignment, qualities valued by society are discussed, positive attributes named, and a personal compilation created by each student. This process alone is valuable as an "exception"-building activity. By looking at all of these qualities, students build personal **potentials.**

Renée Traczyk, special education teacher, used this idea and found, "Additionally, when a problem would arise during the seventh and eighth grade, if necessary, we could get out the hero book and reread the hero paper, discussing how that person might handle the current problem situation. Many good ideas would result" (quote used with permission from Renée Traczyk). Wayne Crick, secondary science teacher, commented, "Today's 'heroes' are not what they used to be, and students may be lacking in this area. If this is the case, perhaps using assignments where students can create their own hero is not only helpful but very necessary" (quote used with permission from Wayne Crick).

May I Help You?

Sometimes taking responsibility means asking for or using help or both—finding and using resources, networking, getting assistance, or using support systems. Two things can be accomplished when we discuss who or what can help students with solutions. We illustrate, first, that it is OK, and sometimes necessary, to get help, and second, how to do it. This step is finalized during the **plan.** When discussing exceptions or pretending a solution, the advice and modeling of others may have come up. It could be that, in the past, people have been helpful when the problem occurred less or not at all. Maybe present exceptions involve others.

"A word of caution: People resources have to be just that—resources" (Webb, 1999, p. 112). Reminding students that they cannot control others is crucial. The solution to the problem cannot be her mother getting nicer again, his friend letting him win at soccer, or the teacher changing the rules. People resources are things like a tutor, a parent who helps as a reminder, someone to share the **plan** with, or a teacher who answers questions. The use of the resources has to be dependent on students. They have to take the initiative to ask for help, for reminders, for support. MASTER 19 "Language Lesson: People Potential" will get you on your way with some helpful questions and phrases to use in leading students toward responsible assistance.

People Potential

MASTER 19

As Models for **Potential** Solutions

How would your friends solve this problem, handle this situation?

What would your parent(s)/guardian(s) do?

What would your positive person/hero do in this situation?

How do others your age deal with this?

What have you seen that works for the other students?

Tell me how (person's name) keeps this from happening.

Describe how (person's name) _____ (e.g., does her work, gets here on time, stays out of fights).

For Advice on **Potential** Solutions

What would I (your teacher) say to you that you could do or try to solve this problem?

What would your parent(s)/guardian(s) want/say?

What would _____ (e.g., the principal, your best friend, your hero, your positive person) suggest to try?

What would (person's name) say works for him or her? Could you ask the person?

What advice do you need? Where could you get it?

What does the school rule/handbook/class policy say you could do?

What might your _____ (e.g., grandfather, mother, other relative) say about this?

For Resources and Support

How might I help you with this?

Who or what can help you?

Who knows what you need to know?

Where can you find the information you need?

Who could support you in working toward your solution?

Who or what has helped you in the past?

Who or what helps you now?

How might you find someone to help?

Could you find a resource that could help your solution happen?

SOURCE: Adapted from *Solutioning: Solution-Focused Interventions for Counselors* (p. 113), by W. Webb, 1999, Philadelphia: Taylor and Francis/Accelerated Development. Used with permission.

Add your own here:

LANGUAGE LESSON

What About "I Don't Knows," Shrugs, and Other Unproductive Responses?

One question asked in all workshops is "What do you do when the student just keeps saying, 'I don't know'?" Two common circumstances seem to be behind the question. The first circumstance is that many educators are accustomed to brainstorming as used in traditional problem-solving methods. The typical brainstorm expects students to pull solution alternatives out of thin air. If students already knew solutions, they would be in current use. This process brings resistance, frustration, and a lack of cooperation often illustrated with shrugs, "I don't knows," and other unproductive responses. My workshop participants used to this type of interaction think it is a possibility with solutioning as well. However, that does not usually prove to be the case. Because of the specificity of the **potentials** questions and the way they are used to construct solutions, students are not asked to come up with information they are not capable of accessing. We must remember that our students are children (even those almighty seniors) and have limited experience in the world. Considering times when problems are less intense, pretending a desired tomorrow, or examining examples of others is very much within their abilities (even kindergartners). Solutioning feeds the brainstorm, so to speak, thus reducing the shrugs. Additionally, with several **potentials** questions under your belt, you will just move on to the next when you get an "I don't know," which is sometimes an honest answer and very acceptable response, not indicative of resistance.

The second circumstance is that the person asking has had many conversations/problem-solving discussions with students who did not share the problem/**purpose** in the beginning. Solutioning emphasizes including students as responsible partners in the process and is flexible. If resistance, shrugs, or a lack of cooperation is apparent during the search for **potential** solutions, go back and spend a little more time developing a *joint purpose.* Does the student have the problem, or does the educator? Would a look at consequences (both positive and negative) motivate the student? Has the student lost hope?

Another alternative for uncooperative silence is given in Chapter 4—cocreating **plans** that fit students. Some students have a difficult time seeing out from under their problems; others have been so encompassed that it is almost impossible for them to consider a better tomorrow. Solutioning adjusts to the readiness of students and incorporates the time needed for change with various **plan** options. Remember the ripple quality of change. Patience, as all educators know, is an asset in all interactions with students, even solutioning.

Keeping Score

A written record of the **potential** solutions discovered is not only helpful during the planning stage to follow but also a great self-esteem builder (Webb, 1999). As a great skill/**potential** solution comes up, accentuate it by saying,

"Let's get this down" (Webb, 1999). Then jot down a two- or three-word summary. When students see the list of exceptions to their problem and **potentials** they have for solutions, they really seem to gain self-confidence and motivation to overcome the problem, which doesn't seem quite so huge anymore (Webb, 1999).

Another advantage to a visual display of abilities and **potential** solutions is that, from then on, it is very difficult for the students to continue to have the problem (Webb, 1999). We've all had those students who put a lot of effort into having their problems and very little effort into solving them. These students are found out, so to speak, when a written list of things they can do to solve the problem (that they shared) is available. After it is out in the open, they no longer can use the problem for an excuse (Webb, 1999). For students with really low self-esteem, it's like seeing is believing. They don't believe they have the ability to overcome the problem (yet) but can't argue with a list of skills and **potentials** they have discovered. A common response is, "Wow, I didn't know I could do all that." Steer clear of forms with lines for this type of list; the emphasis on what the student can do is decreased when blank lines are left over. In that case, a subtle message might be that the student cannot do enough. The nearest piece of paper works best. Grab it, after an exception or **potential** is shared, as if the **potential** is so great that you just have to write it down. A pause and a message of "Wait a minute. This is good stuff. We better write it down so we don't forget" is very effective (Webb, 1999).

As you are first becoming comfortable with solutioning, a form with the questions and a space to write may be helpful. When the form has limited space for writing answers, using the back of the sheet makes students feel exceptional because they have more **potentials** than there was room for on the form. (An example is MASTER 20 "Student Worksheet: Potentials.") Remember, you don't have to ask every question, and write big so that you'll have **potentials** overflow.

Teresa

After many moves, going back and forth between Mom and Dad, some bouts with depression, and a suicide attempt, now Teresa was failing my English class and the eighth grade. After talking about anger (externalized problem), which she thought was her biggest problem right now, drawing some scales, and making some lists of what created anger, we began to look at **potentials.**

Teresa: I get so mad when me and my mom fight.

W.W.: When don't you and your mom fight?

> Teresa looked surprised. She thought we were going to talk about when they do fight. She thought for a moment.

Teresa: When we're just talking.

W.W.: Just talking, that sounds nice. What do you talk about when you are "just talking"? (clarify exception; I asked this as I wrote down "just talking")

Teresa: Like about something we have in common. When we talk about shopping or the cat or something.

W.W.: Cool. When else do you and your mom get along? (positive representation of not fighting)

Teresa's demeanor began to improve as she thought of good times with Mom, as opposed to her previous focus on everything bad and horrible about her life.

Teresa: Sometimes when we start to fight, I'll just change the subject to something safe, like laundry. I like to do laundry.

W.W.: Oo, that's a good one. Let me get that down, "Change the subject." So that works, and you and your mom don't fight but get along, and you don't feel as angry. I didn't know you could do that. What else do you do that works?

Teresa: (now smiling some) When I get to go with Mom to work in the mornings, it's pretty fun. I help her fix VCRs, and she pays me. We get along then. (now she is using the positive representation)

W.W.: OK, let's add that to the list, "Working together." Great. What else?

Teresa: (thinks for a while) Those are the only ones I can think of right now. (leaves the door open for more **potentials**—on her own)

W.W.: This is awesome. Look at all the things *you* do so that you and your mom can get along and anger can't bother you. Let's try an experiment. Want to? (she nods) Let's see whether you can use one of these skills that you already have, that has worked before, and get along with Mom until Friday. (she makes an unsure face) That's 4 days. (she nods, and I hold up the list so that she can see it and read it and hears all of her **potential** solutions again) Just talking, changing the subject, going to work together in the mornings.

Teresa: Yeah, only 4 days. I'll use changing the subject, and I bet we can get along until Friday.

W.W.: (I put a star next to "change the subject" on the list and gave it to Teresa) We'll talk again on Friday.

On Friday, Teresa rated anger even higher on her scale (which meant better) than she had wanted to be (a real accomplishment for a girl who usually wallowed in misery)! She said that she and her mom hadn't gotten into one fight. A few times they almost did, but Teresa changed the subject and they just talked instead. She said that at those times there really was no reason to fight anyway and that it was a lot less upsetting not to. Of course, a person can't change the subject for the rest of his or her life, and I'm sure they fought again. What solution Teresa really seemed to learn through solutioning, however, is that she does have power over her problems, thus ending her victim stance and helping her take control in many other areas of her life as well.

Students begin to realize their potential,   **Chapter 3 Focused**
and the solution becomes obvious.

The search for **potentials** is a very hope-filled and motivating conversation to have with students. It is more than a brainstorming or problem-solving session. By exploring *past, present, pretend,* and/or *people,* you codiscover what works. These form the basis of not only solutions but also self-esteem and confidence. Despite the many avenues for **potentials** shared, the actual exploration is often very short. In a few short questions, students begin to realize their **potentials** and the solution becomes obvious. The answers to the questions lead right into a **plan.**

Exceptions and **potentials,** the heart of the solutioning focus, prove that problems do not occur 100% of the time, that problems are not invincible, and that the future can be different. There is no talk of causes, blaming, or excuses; this decreases the time involved tremendously. Most important, as you explore with students exceptions and **potential** solutions, you consistently send them the message that the solution will happen and that they can do it but that they are given the choice and the responsibility to do so.

Potentials

MASTER 20

PAST

When has the problem not happened? What were you doing differently?

_____

_____

When in the past has the problem been less? What was different?

_____

_____

_____

When have you been successful in the past? How did you do that?

_____

_____

_____

PRESENT

When is the problem not happening now? What are you doing differently?

_____

_____

_____

During what times are you successful now? How do you do that?

_____

_____

_____

MASTER 20 Continued

When is the problem less or the solution happening a bit?

_____

_____

_____

PRETEND

Pretend your problem is solved. What are you doing?

_____

_____

_____

Visualize your solution. Tell me all the details of what you are doing/saying/feeling/thinking.

_____

_____

_____

Imagine things are how you want them to be. What are you doing?

_____

_____

_____

(continued)

Potentials

MASTER 20 Continued

PEOPLE

What ideas for solutions can you get from others? What do they do?

_____

_____

_____

Who has had this problem before and solved it? How did he or she do it?

_____

_____

_____

How would others your age/your positive person/parent(s) solve this problem?

_____

_____

_____

SUMMARY OF POTENTIAL SOLUTIONS

_____

_____

_____

4

Journey Through Solutioning Plan

Now that you have established a **purpose** and explored/created exceptions and **potential** solutions, it is time to define an achievable **plan.** The solution, the desired state, the thing to do, may already be obvious. "With this step, you merely, but very importantly, firm up the actions and behaviors, set up a time frame for monitoring **progress,** and increase the chances for a positive outcome through additional rehearsal/practice" (Webb, 1999, p. 127). Although referred to as a **plan,** use words that work for you. Some students really respond to the word *goal.* Others need *experiments, contests, a direction, a new trend, preference,* and so on. In any words, it is time to lead students in creating **plans** to take some steps toward solving the problem. "The Plan is the solution or the part of the solution that [students] begin trying immediately" (Webb, 1999, p. 127).

On the Journey Through Solutioning Map (Figure 4.1), you'll notice the **plans** flowing from the **potentials.** A **plan** comes directly out of the **potentials** the student just shared. For those not ready to do something different or to perform, there are *positive* and *practice plan* choices (following). Most students do not want more directives or an "expert" adult telling them what to do. Solutioning strives to empower students by giving them authority over their own behavior and by encouraging responsibility for solutions. We as educators can help create interventions for change and still give students choice, self-control, and responsibility. The **plan** must be created collaboratively, not be something educators force on students. Notice the subtle yet powerful differences in Chart 4.1.

Just as we individualize instruction, we individualize solutions. Student readiness varies with the individual and the situation. To assess student readiness, just ask. Feelings about the **potentials** discovered may or may not be evident. Students may have reasons for being uneasy about change. They may be anxious to do the solution. The only way to know is to ask. When you are clear on just what students are ready to do and because these are never the

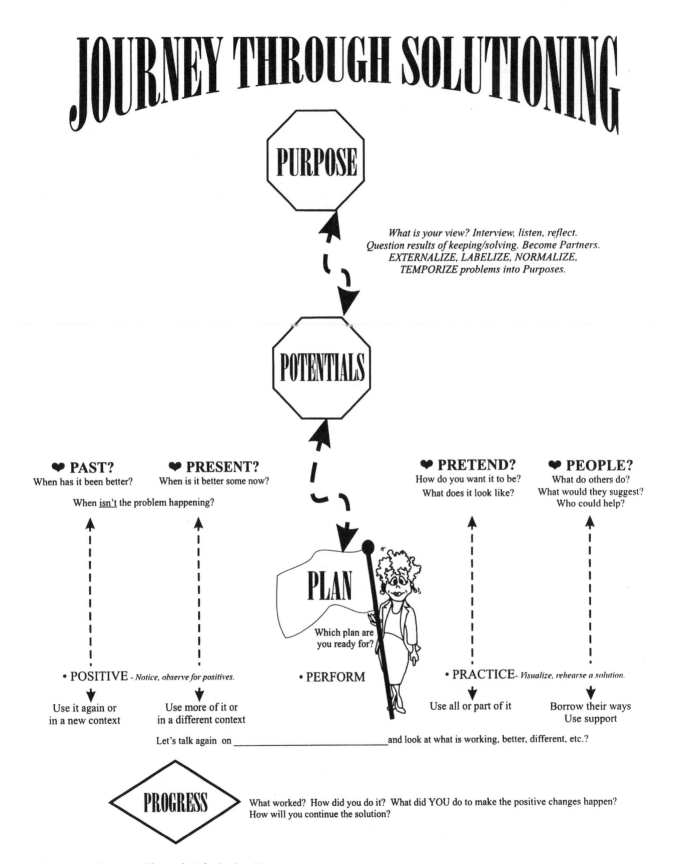

JOURNEY THROUGH SOLUTIONING

PURPOSE

What is your view? Interview, listen, reflect.
Question results of keeping/solving. Become Partners.
EXTERNALIZE, LABELIZE, NORMALIZE,
TEMPORIZE problems into Purposes.

POTENTIALS

❤ **PAST?**
When has it been better?

❤ **PRESENT?**
When is it better some now?

When <u>isn't</u> the problem happening?

❤ **PRETEND?**
How do you want it to be?
What does it look like?

❤ **PEOPLE?**
What do others do?
What would they suggest?
Who could help?

PLAN
Which plan are
you ready for?

• POSITIVE - *Notice, observe for positives.*

• PERFORM

• PRACTICE- *Visualize, rehearse a solution.*

Use it again or
in a new context

Use more of it or
in a different context

Use all or part of it

Borrow their ways
Use support

Let's talk again on _____ and look at what is working, better, different, etc.?

PROGRESS   What worked? How did you do it? What did YOU do to make the positive changes happen?
How will you continue the solution?

Figure 4.1. Journey Through Solutioning Map.

Chart 4.1 The Plan

Problem-Focused, Traditional	Solutioning-Focused
"Now you will . . ."	"What **potentials** do you choose to use?"
"The **plan** is . . ."	"Are you ready to do the solution? Do you need to look for more positives/**potentials** or practice mentally first?"
Tell students what the **plan** will be.	Ask students their choice of a **plan.**
Assign	Collaborate/negotiate
Make a **plan** statement.	Invite a **plan** creation.
Authority	Partnership
Given	Chosen
Control	Responsibility

same, solutioning provides three broad-based **plans** (see Chart 4.2) from which students may choose as they work toward and actualize solutions.

Focus students' attention toward the future and create expectations of success and positive change.

Super Sleuth: The Positive Plan

The *positive plan* develops the solutioning focus and should be used on a regular basis. It can be used as the **plan** itself or in conjunction with others. Observing for positives is useful when you have students who can't quite figure out what their problem really is. Why spend a lot of time finding out what the big problem really is (e.g., why she or he is not successful, hates spelling)? Instead, spend that time and energy looking for when there is success (e.g., when spelling is a little more tolerable) and find some keys to solutions (never knowing, or needing to define a problem). Using solutioning and giving students the responsibility of looking for when problems are absent or are better is not only a more productive use of students' time and energy but also the skill they need to find solutions.

Positive plans help students break away from "problem-saturated descriptions of their lives and relationships" (White & Epston, 1990, p. 16). These "problem-saturated" students have a very difficult time coming up with any **potentials** and just don't seem clear on what action to take, much less ready to do so. When used as the sole **plan,** the time frame for follow-up is small. Every situation is different, so find a time frame that will give students a chance to notice something positive in their lives, but not too long to let them be overcome by the problem again. In other words, try to catch the window of opportunity where students will find some positives/exceptions and be in a state of mind for coming up with a solution **plan.**

Choosing the *positive plan* is an attempt to gain a more hopeful outlook on their situation, feel better and ready for solutions. A word of caution: Do not encourage this for a student you do not think is going to find any positives!

Chart 4.2   Solutioning Plans

Positive	Practice	Perform
1. "Observe for positives." (Walter & Peller, 1992) Notice what works. (Metcalf, 1995) Watch for when things are better.	1. Don't do anything yet, just imagine yourself doing the solution. Visualize doing a **plan**.	1. Do *past potentials* again or in new contexts. 2. Do *present potentials* more or in other contexts. 3. Do all or part of the *pretend potentials*. 4. Borrow some of the *people potentials* to do.

SOURCE: Adapted from *Solutioning: Solution-Focused Interventions for Counselors* (p. 128), by W. Webb, 1999, Philadelphia: Taylor and Francis/Accelerated Development. Used with permission.

What could be more depressing than attempting to find something that works in life and coming up empty, further convinced of the seriousness and hopelessness of the problem(s)? Knowing your students is very helpful.

Another use of the *positive plan* is in conjunction with *practice plans* and *perform plans* (following). Almost like an afterthought, say, "Notice what works" (Metcalf, 1995), "Watch for what goes right," or "Stop and take note when something positive happens." This sends students off with a solutioning focus. "Whether the problem is completely solved or not, usually some efforts are successful/positive. It is the positive change, the small improvement, or the growth that we want to stand out in their minds" (Webb, 1999, p. 136). Students come back and say things like, "Hey, I noticed that I turn in my work better when I study with a friend," or, "I realized that I'm happier when I don't fight with my mom," or, "I found out that my day goes better when I get to school on time." What a great skill to give students (in addition to the solution itself)! Not only are we practicing focusing on and observing for positives as part of *our* focus, but we are also teaching students to do the same. Happier classrooms are the result, classrooms where a great deal of learning can and does take place.

The many phrases that can be used in creating a *positive plan* are in MASTER 21 "Language Lesson: Positive Plans." Some are worded as directives but are not to sound like an assignment. By this point, it is clear for students that we are not giving them another lecture, disciplining, or directing. A partnership has been formed, and the statements come across as words of encouragement, rather than as directives. Focus students' attention toward the future and create expectations of success and positive change.

Positive Plans

MASTER 21

Look for what is good about your life.

Watch for when things are better.

Don't do anything for 3 days; just notice what works.

Watch for things you want to continue doing.

See whether you can find any times when the solution is happening.

Find times when the problem is absent or not as bad.

Remember what happens, between now and when we discuss this again, that you want to keep happening in your life so that you can tell me about it.

Notice what works.

List what is good/works about _____ (e.g., school, life, **plan,** goal).

When your **plan** seems to be working, stop and see what you're doing.

Between today and tomorrow, focus on what's happening that you want to continue.

SOURCE: Adapted from de Shazer, 1985; Metcalf, 1995; and Webb, 1998.

Observe for Positives: Becoming Solution-Focused in Brief Therapy

Between now and the next time you come in, we would like you to look out for those times when there is some harmony in the family (clients' goal) and take note of what you and everyone else are doing. It seems you must be doing something right at those times and we would like to know more about what that might be. (Walter & Peller, 1992, p. 126)

Add your own here:

LANGUAGE LESSON

**Get Ready: The
Practice Plan**

*When students are playing the right pictures
in their minds, solutions happen.*

The *practice plan* plants the seeds of solution. With some nurturing, mainly time, the behavior blooms. The *practice plan* allows you truly to individualize, acknowledging varying degrees of student readiness. Much of the practice here is done mentally. Epstein (1990) defines *mental imagery* as "the mind thinking in pictures" (p. 11). When students are playing the right pictures in their minds, solutions happen. The first step is getting them to play the right pictures, which is the **purpose** of the *practice plan.* According to Goldberg (1995), by encouraging the mental rehearsal of solutions, you are giving students "blueprints for actions and behaviors" (p. 24). The *practice plan* involves the thinking and feeling that precedes the behavior (Webb, 1999). Children and adolescents sometimes have to rehearse, practice, and prepare before than can take action. Of course, it is helpful to tie the **plan** into an already existing behavior or success. When this is not possible, the *practice plan* is an effective choice and can be used to practice any **potentials** discovered (not just pretend ones). The use of visualization allows students to take solutions into their lives without risk and to build up the confidence necessary for actualization (Webb, 1999).

Encouraging students to think about doing their solution results in private, personal, mental rehearsal of the desired, positive behavior. The **plan** is to do nothing except think about, pretend, or mentally practice the solution (see MASTER 22 "Language Lesson: Practice Plans"), although the behavior often follows as it did with Ashley, a student with whom I consulted in my private practice:

"Hi"

Ashley was a fifth-grader who had an older sister in high school. Ashley's dream in life was to be popular like her sister. However, Ashley was overweight and shy. She had been teased a lot and often used obstinacy as a defense when people tried to interact with her. These qualities, as you can imagine, made popularity seem like a distant goal. During solutioning, however, Ashley was quickly able to share **potential** solutions when asked, "Who has solved this problem that you could get ideas from?" She just thought of her sister, who had not been popular in the early grades because of shyness but who was now outgoing and busy with friends and activities. Ashley described many positive behaviors that were modeled by her sister. When asked the **plan** question, "Which of these great ideas are you going to try first?" Ashley looked uncomfortable and thought for a moment. She then shared that maybe she could start saying "Hi" to other students/potential friends when she saw them at school. Because of her hesitation, I asked, "Are you ready? Is it worth the risk?" Ashley wasn't sure, so we used the *practice plan* to find out.

Ashley decided that she would not do anything yet, just imagine herself smiling and saying "Hi" each time she passed a potential friend in the hall or during lunch. We decided she should use the mental rehearsal for 1 week, and we'd see how she felt about it then. Ashley came back thrilled because she had actually said "Hi" to two girls that very day before the session. They had each said "Hi" back, hadn't ignored her or laughed at her or made fun of her at all. Ashley commented as we considered her **progress,** "I knew I wasn't supposed to do anything yet, just practice in my mind, but I got so good at the practice, it just came out. I couldn't resist."

SOURCE: *Solutioning: Solution-Focused Interventions for Counselors* (pp. 140-141), by W. Webb, 1999, Philadelphia: Taylor and Francis/Accelerated Development. Used with permission.

Practice Plans

MASTER 22

For the next 2 days, imagine yourself (describe the solution behavior) when the problem is trying to take over. Notice how you feel.

EXAMPLES:

For the next 2 days, imagine yourself taking a deep breath when you feel like looking at your neighbor's paper for the answers.

From now until Monday, imagine yourself putting your books into your backpack before you go to bed at night.

Pretend you tell your English teacher that you need some extra help with paragraphs when you get frustrated with your essay.

Visualize yourself asking your parents to get you a tutor each time you see them for the next 3 days. Notice how you feel.

Do absolutely nothing until we talk again. Just think about/imagine doing your solution, but don't do anything yet.

EXAMPLES:

Do nothing, just think about getting to school on time for a few days. Remember, don't come to school on time yet.

Just think about walking in the halls, but remember not to yet.

For 2 days, don't control your anger, just think about your **plan** of being able to take two deep breaths and walk into the gym when the guys tease you.

Remember when the girls call you a name to keep getting upset, but while you're upset imagine yourself blowing them off and walking over to your other friends.

LANGUAGE LESSON

Practice Plans

MASTER 22 Continued

Practice your solution in your mind each time your problem comes up (e.g., before bed, first thing in the morning). Think about which part you'll do first.

Play your solution movie each time you feel tempted to _____ (e.g., cheat, be angry, be sad, be scared).

For a few days, think about how you are going to act/feel/think differently when you decide to do your solution.

> Have them pretend that they are operating a VCR in their mind. When a negative image pops up, they need to hit the stop button, rewind, and then play the scene again. If it comes up negative a second or third time, have them repeat it or even put the movie in slow motion, until they play it right. (Goldberg, 1995, p. 25)

Add your own here:

SOURCE: *Solutioning: Solution-Focused Interventions for Counselors* (p. 144), by W. Webb, 1999, Philadelphia: Taylor and Francis/Accelerated Development. Used with permission.

LANGUAGE LESSON

Lights, Camera, Action: The Perform Plan

As you'll notice on the Journey Through Solutioning Map (Figure 4.1), if you follow down directly from each type of **potential**, you have an automatic plan—reusing, increasing, or trying a behavior. The idea is to *perform*. In traditional methods, the teacher tells the students the solution (the answer, the correction, the reprimand, the way it's going to be) in the very beginning. Solutioning's way of using a few well-formed questions, however, results in students telling the teacher how they are going to solve the problem (make things right, different, better; Webb, 1999). The **plan**/solution comes directly from the exceptions to the problem and **potential** solutions students just discovered, building in confidence, ownership, and responsibility. Sometimes, after an enlightening discussion of exceptions/**potentials,** it is tempting to just say, "OK, now go for it," ending the conversation there. This usually works, but taking a few more minutes and allowing students to tell you what they are going to *choose to do* works better (Webb, 1999).

Karen

Journal entry of Kathy Lemon, fifth- through seventh-grade counselor/teacher (Used with permission from Kathy Lemon)

Karen is a 12-year-old adopted twin in fifth grade. She is not accepted by classmates because of her lack of social skills. She has become a victim of ridicule and teasing. In the beginning, I assigned ways for her to improve skills, interaction techniques, and even gave her homework in hopes of a "quick fix" for her. I talked with others to encourage them to give her the opportunity to use her skills. She was opposed to some techniques I recommended because she was unwilling to help herself. It was as though she enjoyed the negative treatment so that she had a reason to come to me and have me feel sorry for her.

After I began taking this (solutioning) class and changed my way of interacting with her, she refused to comply with the method of taking responsibility for herself at first. When I asked her the questions, she said the teasing was the worst when she tattled on others or yelled at them. I asked her when things were best, and she said when she was alone playing with her sister or working alone in the classroom. I asked her what she could do to make the problem better in the class, and she was unwilling to answer the question. I think she wants to avoid any answer that would take the blame off the others and focus on her own behavior. What she really wants is for her teacher and me to solve all of her difficulties for her by making the others leave her alone. If that doesn't work for her, then she can blame me for failing her, rather than blame herself.

Karen reported that the problem was better when she didn't tattle but that she didn't want to stop tattling because she thought it was her job to tell the teacher. She also said that it was better when she didn't yell at others. Of the two things, she *chose* to stop yelling, rather than stop tattling. She said that her **plan** was to stop yelling even if others annoyed her.

When we talked again, Karen said that she didn't yell at her classmates as much and that she had decided also not to tattle as much unless the children were really doing bad things. When I told her the teacher had said that the children hadn't picked on Karen as much and that her overall behavior and the behavior of others had improved, she finally validated what the teacher had said and admitted things were better. She finally took credit that it was because of things she had done differently! Wow, what a difference. We could have played the pity, blame game all year, and now she is taking a little responsibility. Choice made the difference. I wanted to tell her not to yell or tattle, but I let her pick her own **plan** to perform; as a result, she did both.

Perform Plans

MASTER 23

GENERAL

Of all the skills you've shared with me today, which will you choose as your solution?

Well, John, we've talked about a lot of **potential** solutions. Which one are you going to be choosing/using?

It seems clear, Mali, that by (describe behaviors that have been discussed that work), you are able to (**purpose**/goal). It's great that you'll be _____ (e.g., coming to school on time, talking to me respectfully).

Example: "It seems clear, Mali, that by putting your hands in your pockets you are able to control pushing. It's great that you'll be getting to go out to recess now."

PAST

Of the things that have worked for you before, which might you use again now?

Wow, in the past when you (describe behavior), it really seemed to work. I am excited that you can begin doing it again now.

Example: "Wow, in the past when you told yourself to calm down, it really seemed to work. I am excited that you will be doing it again."

PRESENT

So, it sounds like by doing what works for you sometimes, even more of the time, you will solve your problem. Cool.

Now that you know that when you (describe behavior) things are better, you can do it more.

Example: "Now that you know when you sit away from friends things are better, you can sit there all the time."

LANGUAGE LESSON

Perform Plans

MASTER 23 Continued

PRETEND

Which part of your pretend solution are you going to begin doing tomorrow?

Now that you know how you want things to be, you can start making them that way. Which part will you do first?

PEOPLE

Which part of so and so's successful behavior (describe it) are you going to try?

Example: "Which part of Rosa's study skills (e.g., saying the words aloud, making flash cards, practicing with a friend) are you going to try first?"

Of all the things you've shared that others might suggest, which are you going to choose?

Add your own here:

LANGUAGE LESSON

**Observable, Doable,
Achievable**

*Answers to positively stated questions form a
mental rehearsal of the desired behavior.*

No matter which type of **plan** is used, it has to be observable, doable, and achievable—or why bother? Too often, educators send students off to do unrealistic **plans,** students set goals with little idea of how to get there, or a **plan**'s success is contingent on factors out of students' control. Avoid these traps with carefully worded questions for a **plan** that is *personal, positive, process, present,* and *precise*—Fab Five criteria guaranteed for success.

The first quality, *personal,* means within students' control. **Plans** that involve someone else changing first or that are contingent in any way on circumstances over which students have no control rarely succeed. Many times, students cannot see past their desire for the other children or their parents to get off their backs, for their teacher to teach differently, or for their math to get easier. These are repercussions of the blame game. If the problem is always someone else's fault, then the solution must involve them changing. Simply question students about the likelihood of changing their friends, parents, teachers, math, or state: "We cannot control anyone but ourselves. Now what can *you* do?"

When students are having difficulty personalizing solution possibilities and forming **plans** that involve behaviors for them alone, you may ask the following questions as adapted from the "key words" suggested by Walter and Peller (1992):

"What will *you* be doing *instead?*"
"What will/could *you* be doing *differently?*"
"What would so and so (e.g., teacher, parent, peer) say *you* could do?"
"Which of the **potentials** we have discussed could *you* try?"

Through the use of words like *instead* and *differently,* we have also met the positive quality. For a moment, close your eyes and imagine yourself not eating a piece of cherry pie. Did you see cherry pie in there somewhere? We don't want students visualizing the problem behavior each time they think of their solution (Webb, 1999). Students have to form **plans** that positively state what they will be doing, as opposed to what they will not be doing. Some of the best intended goals and **plans** never happen because the student didn't know what to do. **Plans** of not failing, of not getting detention, of not forgetting homework are fine if the details of how not to do these things and what to do instead are discussed. The answers to positively stated questions form a mental rehearsal of the desired behavior.

Questions can also be used to encourage students to create **plans** that involve the doing of the solution, emphasizing *process.* End states, wishes, and desires do not enable results; behaviors do. The idea here is to create a movielike view of the solutions (Webb, 1999). Using *how* and *-ing* verbs will make the **plan** doable and observable (Walter & Peller, 1992):

> "*How* will you be *doing* this?" (after a desire)
> "*How* will you be *passing?*" (after an end state)
> "*How* will you be *getting* here on time?"
> "*How* will you be *making* friends?" (after a wish)
> "*How* will you be *controlling* your emotions?"

Additional qualities of doable **plans** are *precise* and *present*. These may have already been met in answering the questions above. However, when students are having a difficult time forming an achievable **plan** or when you think that more details and rehearsal would be helpful, think of these qualities. "By asking for details, the **plan** is made more precise, more movielike, more specific, and therefore more achievable" (Webb, 1999, p. 149).

> "How, specifically, will you be doing this?"
> "Now, exactly what are you going to be doing?"
> "Tell it to me like a movie . . . "
> "What does it look like?"
> "I want all the details of your **plan.** What will you be doing?"

Notice the emphasis on *you* (personal) and *doing* (process and positive). A nice example of the "What does it look like?" question comes from the following section of Jo Johnston's journal.

Lucy

Journal entry of Jo Johnston, middle school physical education/health teacher (Used with permission from Jo Johnston)

I asked her if there was something she could do so that the other students would like her.

Lucy: Oh, ya. I could be nice and polite and stuff.

J.J.: What would that look like, you being nice and polite and stuff?

Lucy: I really don't know. It's been so long.

J.J.: How long has it been?

Lucy: Probably last Christmas, when I was nice even though I didn't get what I wanted.

J.J.: Lucy, what exactly does nice and polite look like?

Lucy: Oh, I don't say mean things, and I say please and thank you—you know, polite.

During this dialogue, Lucy realized exactly what she could do to have better relationships as she moved to a new school. By describing the behaviors, the **plan** is more doable. Notice that Ms. Johnston had to re-ask the question, and it paid off. Students are not used to solutioning language and may have to hear it more than once.

Finally, **plans** need to involve actions to begin immediately in the present. What good is a **plan** to graduate when the student is currently a seventh grader? What good is a **plan** to get on the honor roll when the student is currently failing two classes? These are valid long-term goals, but for students to begin making changes, **plans** for *now* must be created (Webb, 1999). The following questions can help students bring their **plans** into the present:

"When you come to class tomorrow and you are on-track, what will you be doing differently or saying differently to yourself?" (adapted from Walter & Peller, 1992)

"Starting tomorrow, when you're on your way toward the honor roll (end solution), what will you be doing?"

"From now on, when you're in the groove and coming to school on time, how will you be doing it?"

"When you're on the road to controlling your anger, what will you be doing/feeling/saying instead?"

Many of these questions have elements that satisfy all of the five qualities. The **plan** stage of the conversation does not need to be complicated. On the contrary, it is usually the most obvious, motivated, and exciting part. MASTER 24 "Language Lesson: The Fab Five Plan Criteria" and MASTER 25 "Practice Makes Perfect: Plans" will help you and your students turn vague, unclear, or negative desires/goals into **plans** that will happen. This is a life skill for students that is usable even when problems don't exist.

The Fab Five Plan Criteria

MASTER 24

Through questioning, you can assist the student in cocreating a **plan** that is observable and doable. This encourages the visualization of the desired outcome (solution), increasing the chances that it will happen!

1. **PERSONAL** In the student's control and language	*you*	"What will *you* be saying (doing, thinking)?"
		"So, when you chill out first you can . . ."
2. **POSITIVE**	*instead*	"What will you be doing *instead* of cheating on the test?"
	differently	"What will you be doing *differently* when you are on time to class?"
3. **PROCESS**	*how, -ing*	"*How* will you be do*ing* this?" "*How* will you be turning in work?"
4. **PRECISE**	*specifically* *exactly*	"How, *specifically*, will you . . . ?" "What, *exactly*, will you do?" "What does it look like?"
5. **PRESENT**	*on-track*	"When you come to class tomorrow and you are *on-track*, what will you be doing differently or saying differently to yourself?"

SOURCE: Adapted from *Becoming Solution-Focused in Brief Therapy*, (p. 60), by J. L. Walter and J. E. Peller, 1992, New York: Bruner-Mazel.

LANGUAGE LESSON

Practice Makes Perfect

PLANS

MASTER 25

Co-create the following student's **plans** so that they are observable, doable, and achievable. What questions would lead students toward the creation of success?

FOR EXAMPLE:

1. Laila: "I want to stop getting kicked out of your class every day."

QUESTIONS TO ASK:

"Laila, what will *you* be do*ing instead* of being kicked out?"

"Tomorrow when *you* come to class and *you're on-track* to stay*ing* in class all hour, what exactly will you be do*ing differently?*"

NEW PLAN:

I will follow directions in class and work on my assignments instead of yelling at the other kids.

2. Gino: "I want to get out of special ed."

QUESTIONS TO ASK:

_____

_____

NEW PLAN:

_____

_____

_____

_____

Practice Makes Perfect

PLANS

MASTER 25 Continued

3. Christina: "I wish the other kids liked me."

QUESTIONS TO ASK:

_____

_____

NEW PLAN:

_____

_____

_____

_____

4. Paul: "I just want to do good in school."

QUESTIONS TO ASK:

_____

_____

NEW PLAN:

_____

_____

_____

_____

Double the Odds   *The simplicity of solutioning need not be undersold by the numerous*
examples, samples, and things to try. It is effective to have a full bag
of solutioning-focused language and ideas to use as needed.

No matter how obvious the solution, how achievable the **plan,** the following techniques will increase the odds for success, ease student fears, and increase motivation.

- *Assume success* by using "presuppositional language" (O'Hanlon, 1996).
- *Make it emotional* by discussing the student's feelings about the **plan.**
- *Add supporting roles* by including others as resources, support.
- *Plan the party* by including a developmentally and situationally appropriate time frame for follow-up, monitoring, and noting **progress.**
- *Script success* by putting **plans** in writing.
- *Rehearse out roadblocks* by having the student mentally go over the **plan,** including any possible roadblocks or barriers.

Remember, you do not have to ask every question or use every idea. These are not intended to make the process more time-consuming, but rather to use for all its worth what time and effort is being given. The majority of the time, these will already be covered or can be in one additional sentence or question. Presuppositional language will be evident in all of your questions and statements during the **plan** stage of the process. In fact, you've already experienced it in the Language Lessons.

Assume Success

Choose your words very carefully to show that you know and believe **plans** will happen. You will notice that every question in this chapter uses *when,* not *if,* in referring to the outcome of the **plan/**solution. By using "When the **plan** happens," rather than "If the **plan** happens," you are setting up the student for success. Another good word to use is *after*—for example, "After you take the test without cheating, I want you to tell me all about it." Never use words like *might* or *may,* but strong "doing" verbs like *will* and *are*—for example, "So, Juan, when you are choosing to talk respectfully to me for the next few days, notice the outcome." A very different message would have been given if you were to say something like, "Juan, you should talk respectfully to me for a few days . . . " or "If you talk respectfully, . . . " The educator's belief in the student (or lack of it) is clearly portrayed with one or two little words.

When . . .

I was once told the story of an elementary school child and a very special principal who used solutioning's idea of presuppositional language. The child had experienced intense abuse and had been selectively mute for the past 6 months. One day, the principal got down next to the little girl and said, "When you start talking, I can't wait to hear what you have to say." This proved a pivotal point for the child, and within 1 month she began speaking.

Make It Emotional

Feeling questions encourage sharing emotions about doing the **plan,** relieve any uneasiness, and increase motivation. When students are telling you their **plans,** stop them at various points and ask, "How are you feeling right now as you tell me about doing this?" "The answer to this question will give a lot of insight into the likelihood of success" (Webb, 1999, p. 153). Another advantage of feeling questions is the rehearsal. When students go off to do their **plans,** very few surprises should await them. Experiencing, even partially, the feelings associated with carrying out solutions will help students know they are prepared and ready.

When the feelings are not very positive, a great follow-up question is "Is it worth the risk?" Once again, giving students choice is crucial for responsibility. A student may not be ready for the entire **plan** yet. More practice or trying some of the **plan** may be necessary. This question allows the student to make a good choice now, rather than attempting a **plan** and failing later. When students seem unsure, ask questions like "Are you ready to do it?" or "How do you feel when you imagine yourself doing this **plan?**"

For students who are feeling optimistic toward their **plans,** allowing them the opportunity to share this optimism increases their motivation and excitement to go for it. Although this step can easily be left out and for time's sake often is without negative consequences, it is very effective. A few suggestions for incorporating emotions are in MASTER 26 "Language Lesson: Making It Emotional."

Making It Emotional

MASTER 26

How do you feel when you describe doing your **plan**?

What feelings might come up when you go out to do your **plan**?

What goes on inside you when you imagine yourself (describe it)?

Are you excited, scared, nervous, motivated about _____ ?

Is it worth the risk?

Are you ready?

How are you feeling right now?

How might you feel tomorrow?

Which parts make you feel the most _____ (e.g., excited, nervous)?

What would help you feel _____ (e.g., ready, motivated, confident)?

What would help you feel less _____ (e.g., nervous, scared, unsure)?

Add your own here:

LANGUAGE LESSON

Add Supporting Roles

Extend students' mental movies by including more characters. "Who will be the first person (e.g., teacher, friend, parent) to notice when you _____ _____ (e.g., come to class on time, turn in your work, control your anger)?" Remember to stress that they cannot control how others will react, they can only imagine different possible reactions and see how that might feel or affect their solutions (Webb, 1999). Educators can facilitate students' preparation by helping them consider a variety of outcomes. "What might Takeesha say when you tell her you want to be friends again?" "What is the first thing your parents might do when your grades improve?" Frances Hunt, a master teacher, successfully used the question "How will your speech teacher know you are behaving differently?" to help a third-grader transfer her successful behavior from Mrs. Hunt's class into other areas of school functioning in which the girl was having difficulties.

Other frames of reference also illustrate who can help support the **plan**, allowing these support people to be fully used (see MASTER 27 "Language Lesson: Supporting Roles"). Ask students whom they might share their **plans** with or whom they could ask for help. For example, the "talker" in Chapter 3 had to warn her friends that she would not be talking to them as much anymore so they would not think she was mad at them. This was a crucial step in her success. If she would not have set this up, she could have successfully carried out her **plan** of "controlling talking" but not felt successful because of new problems with friends. By considering the entire picture, she was able to include her friends as part of her **plan** and to increase her support at the same time.

Supporting Roles

MASTER 27

OTHER FRAMES OF REFERENCE:

How might _____ (e.g., peers, parents, myself/teacher) react when you (describe the **plan**)?

What will so and so probably do when you (describe **plan**)?

Who will notice when you (describe the **plan**)?

Who will be the first to know that you have solved your problem? What might she or he say or do?

When so and so realizes that you have solved your problem, what might she or he say/do/feel?

FOR SUPPORT:

Who else do we need to include in this **plan**?

Are you going to tell anyone else about your **plan**?

Who will be your best ally against the problem?

What will be your greatest source of support for completing this **plan**?

Who or what can help you?

Are you going to use any of the people you've used before?

Are there any people who are helping/supporting you now that you can continue with or use even more?

Add your own here:

_____

SOURCE: Adapted from *Solutioning: Solution-Focused Interventions for Counselors* (pp. 155-156), by W. Webb, 1999, Philadelphia: Taylor and Francis/Accelerated Development. Used with permission.

LANGUAGE LESSON

Plan the Party

A time frame for following up, monitoring, and celebrating **progress** should be included. The amount of time given for the **plan** needs to be appropriate not only for the situation but also for students' developmental levels (Webb, 1999). Give enough time for **progress** to be worthy or valid, yet not so much that the sense of success has subsided. Just imagine if we gave students assignments without due dates or completion guidelines. How many assignments do you think would be completed? Following are some guidelines for age-appropriate time frames for follow-up to use when making final **plans**:

K-2nd grade: half a day or less (e.g., an hour, recess)

3rd-4th grade: half a day to 1 day

5th-6th grade: 1 or 2 days (maximum)

7th-8th grade: 2 to 4 days (maximum)

9th-12th grade: 2 days to 1 week (maximum)

Guidelines are helpful, but the best source for determining the amount of time are the students. Continue giving responsibility by asking something like, "When should we get back together and talk about the success of your **plan**?" or "How much time do you think you'll need to find positives, practice, or do your **plan**?"

Script Success

By writing down the **plan,** the students will see it, giving them a visual and perhaps making it more real. In fact, this can be used with difficult cases to encourage the students to take the **plan** more seriously. Writing facilitates agreement on the details of the **plan**. Finally, a written **plan** can easily be referred to during the **progress** stage (Chapter 5). During **progress,** a written account shows students exactly what they did to solve the problem, not just gives them a feeling that the problem is better.

With older students, having them write down the **plan** provides another rehearsal, gives them a feeling of control, and makes the **plan** official. To emphasize the partnership (not like the teacher giving an assignment), both may write down the **plan** and so each has a copy. Younger students can sometimes draw their **plans.** This **plan** is not a blueprint, but a representation of what the students are going to do. Then the educator can write down the steps for them, collaboratively wording it. Involving students here is key. Doing it together is more important than what is actually written (Webb, 1999).

This step is not necessary, and time usually does not allow it. When time is available, however, jot down some form of **plan**. Remember, it does not have to be formal, detailed, and perfect (Webb, 1999). If a list of **potentials** was kept, star the choice, circle the one developed into the **plan,** or add several sentences, and you've got it; just add a time frame for follow-up.

In some situations, the **plan** may need to seem more like a contract, so write it up (or type it on the computer) and then both student and teacher sign it. This is especially useful when using solutioning in conflict mediation (Chapter 7). True to life, you take something a little more seriously if you sign your name to it. Students are no different. MASTER 28 "Success Script" can be your guide. The handiest note pad or piece of scrap paper, however, would serve as well. The freedom of a blank sheet of paper allows the solutioning process to unfold as it happens to come out in that particular situation with that individual student (Webb, 1999).

MASTER 28

Success Script

Date: _____

Names of those involved in this solutioning conversation:

_____

_____

Purpose:

_____

_____

Potentials: _____

_____

_____

Plan: _____

_____

_____

Progress: _____

_____

_____

_____

_____

_____

Rehearse Out Roadblocks

When students still seem unsure or uneasy about their **plans,** it may be helpful to use mental rehearsal, discussing possible barriers to carrying out the **plans.** The idea is to ask students to tell you of any roadblocks they might foresee. Then together you plan how to avoid them, cope with them, or decrease the chance of them happening (Webb, 1999). My adult students call this "dodging roadblocks" or "stopping setbacks." Metcalf (1995) calls it "flagging the minefield." The rehearsal, complete with a **plan** for barriers, is very proactive, motivating, and empowering for students.

By discussing potential roadblocks before they happen, students will be better equipped to handle them when they do happen. In other words, when necessary, you and the students set up possible sabotages and find solutions for them (see MASTER 29 "Language Lesson: Rehearsing Out Roadblocks")—for example, "Do you know of anything that could get in the way of this **plan** happening?" The answers provide the rest. Some students are so confident and motivated by this point that nothing can stop them. Others are a little nervous about actually going out and doing something differently (Webb, 1999).

Fearless Freddy?

After a brief solutioning conversation, Freddy had a **plan** to use some positive self-talk. He was going to repeat in his mind, "I don't want to get in trouble. I can control my anger. He's not worth it," whenever he and Adam had a confrontation. Freddy thought this would give him time to calm down and get control over his impulsive actions, which had resulted in his punching Adam in the nose three times during the past semester. As Freddy was about to go back to class, I asked him, "Is there anything that could get in the way of this **plan** happening?" Freddy looked at me as if I were clueless and said, "Well, if Charity is watching, I'll have to hit him." This added a whole new dimension to our solutioning process, and our conversation continued a little longer. The result was informing Charity of his new power of positive thinking, impressing her, and staying out of fights. This **plan** was complete, and it worked great. Without accounting for that potential roadblock, Freddy would have ended up in another fight for sure.

Don't think you have to ask "Do you know of anything that could get in the way of this **plan** happening?" every time. You'll have a feel for when the **plan** seems a little too simple, too easy, or unlikely to happen. When that is the case, this question will provide the answers students need to create achievable **plans.**

Rehearsing Out Roadblocks

MASTER 29

1. Use mental rehearsal.
2. Be optimistic.
3. Be realistic.
4. Avoid giving ideas of possible problems.
5. If the student does not foresee any possible setbacks or challenges, leave it at that.
6. Empower the student with confidence.
7. Compliment the student's abilities, coping skills, and foresight.
8. Build the student up.
9. Remind the student that you can only control yourself.
10. Let the student know that you believe success will happen but that failure is acceptable.
11. Emphasize that solutioning is a process.

What could make carrying out your **plan**/solution difficult for you?

Do you know of anything that could get in your way?

What is going to be the most challenging part of your solution/**plan?**

Describe for me the scariest/hardest part of your **plan.**

THEN:

Follow through with **potentials**-type questions of how students have handled that type of roadblock in the past, how they handle it now, how they might imagine themselves handling it, or how others overcome obstacles. Use the solutioning process to plan/rehearse how to avoid barriers.

SOURCE: Adapted from *Solutioning: Solution-Focused Interventions for Counselors* (pp. 152-153), by W. Webb, 1999, Philadelphia: Taylor and Francis/Accelerated Development. Used with permission.

LANGUAGE LESSON

A Paradoxical Plan?

If you feel that nothing is working with a student, it may be that efforts at solutions are exacerbating the problem. In that case, try the opposite, or a paradoxical plan:

> Most generally, paradoxical instruction involves prescribing behavior that appears in opposition to the goals being sought, in order actually to move toward them. This may be seen as an inverse to pursuing "logical" courses that lead only to more trouble. (Weakland, Fisch, Watzlawick, & Bodin, 1974, p. 158)

Paradox, though a little risky, can be successfully employed with careful wording. After a student goes home and tells her or his parents that the teacher suggested, or that it was decided by student and teacher together, the student should try really hard not to do her or his homework, the parents may be calling. They may be calling until they give it some time and see the results, which are usually very encouraging.

The idea is to create a "double bind" that encourages **progress** no matter which way the student goes. If the student does not do the homework, she or he is cooperating fully with the **plan** and requests of the teacher (something that was not previously happening); if she or he is resistive enough to go against the **plan** and do the homework anyway, then the grades improve.

Make a List

Leroy was a fun student, always laughing, always positive, and always busy but not with assignments. Leroy was so frustrating because he had so many skills—verbal communication, leadership, creativity—none of which were being reflected by his school performance or grades. He hadn't turned in over half of the assignments all year. We had conferenced, I had talked with his upset and concerned father on the telephone many times, the counselor had talked with Leroy, and nothing changed. This was during my own solutioning development. Leroy was in my office at lunch one day for talking excessively during class. Our conversation went something like this:

W.W.: Leroy, I was wondering if we could talk about your missing assignments.

Leroy: I guess. What do you want to know?

W.W.: Well, I'm confused. You do some of them and do them well. That tells me you are capable. So you are able to do them but are choosing not to and fail, despite the efforts of your dad and me. What kind of grade do you want to have?

Leroy: I don't know. I guess a C would be better, then Dad wouldn't lecture me so much.

W.W.: What would you be doing differently if you were getting a C?

Leroy: I'd be doing my homework, but I refuse to do my homework. I hate doing school at home. I have more important things to do.

I knew that suggesting a **plan** of doing homework (exception) would be futile because it had already been an issue of many conferences this year.

W.W.: Hey, I have an idea. Just so I understand and we have documentation to show your dad, why don't you keep a log of all the things you have to do that are more important than your homework. If you start to run out of things and are considering doing your homework, think really hard and I'm sure you will find something else to do. Could you try that for 3 days, just as an experiment to clear up my confusion?

Leroy: Sure.

W.W.: OK, let's talk again in 3 days. Have your log ready to show me, and explain all the things on it that were more important than your homework. Cool. I'll look forward to seeing it.

This would accomplish one of two things: (a) prove to Leroy that he is indeed in control of whether or not he does his homework (in the past, he had tried to blame it on other circumstances) or (b) prove that the other things he was trying to come up with really weren't more important. Either result should encourage a prioritization and the doing of more homework. I really had nothing to lose; he wasn't doing any homework now, and all other "traditional" interventions had already been tried. I contemplated calling the dad and letting him in on the intervention but choose to wait the 3 days and see what Leroy came up with first.

Three Days Later

W.W.: Hey, Leroy, what did you come up with? Let's look at your log.

Leroy: Well, here it is. The first day, I had to ride my bike for a while, then play some Nintendo, and then watch *Seinfeld,* so you see I couldn't really do any homework. (He was struggling with his reply.) The next day, I rode for a while, played a couple games of Mario Brothers, then did my history questions. I guess I couldn't really think of anything more important to do right then. I knew if I didn't do that assignment, I would get an F on my report card for sure. So that seemed more important than TV. The third day, it was raining, so I couldn't ride my bike. I went in to think of things more important than homework, which I thought would be cake, but I kept thinking of how easy it would be to just do it and get the C. So I just did it, right then when I first got home from school. I finished in time to watch all the shows I like on Thursday night just like I always do, and I didn't have Dad yelling at me the whole time.

W.W.: Wow, so when you sat down to see what was more important to do than homework, you decided homework was pretty important.

Leroy: Yeah, I hate to say it, but when I compared them, those other things didn't really seem worth getting an F and having my dad mad all the time.

W.W.: That is a really cool decision.

Leroy continued to turn in more, but not all, of his homework and did pass my class. He stopped as he came in the door about 3 weeks later and said, "I don't have my homework today. I got a new Nintendo game for raising my grade, and it was more important last night." Before I could respond, he added, "But I think by tonight it won't be as important anymore." Because this paradox was working so well, I responded with, "Well, if it is, make sure you play it instead of doing your homework."

Leroy needed to decide for himself the importance of homework. All he had been hearing in the conferences and through the efforts of his father was that he needed to change, that he wasn't good enough, and that he was a failure. By considering for himself the importance of homework, he made the right decision. He had the ability, and now he was choosing to use it. Also, he was just rebellious enough that if I suggested he not do his homework, it made him want to do it a little bit more.

Paradox is a nonconventional intervention but one appropriately suited to the oppositional mind-set of some students. Give paradoxical instructions on a more general level to be cautious. For example, the team at the Brief Therapy Center, who have a 10-session limit, most routinely stress "going slowly" at the outset of treatment. Later, they respond to a report of improvement with a worried look and the statement, "I think things are moving a bit too fast," which speeds up **progress** with their clients tremendously (Weakland et al., 1974).

An effective use of paradox is with friendship battles, which have been known to disrupt the best learners. Caution students, "Maybe you shouldn't be friends with each other anymore. You just fight too much." They become better friends who don't fight as much, or they really stop being friends, both of which accomplish getting them back to their schoolwork. Interestingly, the inverse circumstance of being better friends is usually the result. One of my adult students told a third-grader not to learn the spelling words because the shock of a 100% on the spelling test would be more than his parents could handle. According to Mary Mills, "He got the 100% just to shock his parents. This proved to him that he could do it, his self-esteem improved, and his spelling grade soared."

Sometimes you're not sure what about the paradox works. Frustrated with the lack of change in a very angry student who often got in fights, I said something like this: "You know what I do when I get mad? I put my thumb and finger together and press really hard. I imagine that I am holding my anger there until I get home and can express it. That's so I can get along here at school and keep my job. It works really well for me, but don't you try it. You can think about it if you want to, but don't try it, OK?" The student only got in one more fight the whole second half of the year (he had been averaging one every 2 weeks). I don't know whether he tried the finger thing, stopped for a moment to think when getting mad, or what. When we talked about fighting again, it was a celebration of how he had controlled his anger and not fought. I asked, "How did you do it?" and he just smiled wide and said, "I don't know. I just didn't fight." I was OK with that. It worked.

Scaling   Scaling questions are a solutioning tool that can be used throughout the entire process. Scaling allows you and the students to attach a value on the externalized problem and to discuss what it would look like if it increased. These values and the behaviors they represent can serve both as a helpful monitoring tool for the **plan** and as the **plan** itself. For example, if a student has a problem with running in the halls, the teacher could ask:

Educator: Rate the problem, 1 being the ultimate worst it could be (constant running), and 10 being the best it could be (no running). Where are you now?

1	2	3	4	5	6	7	8	9	10
Running all the time			X						Never running

The student says a 4.

Educator: So, you're at a 4. Where would you like to be by tomorrow?

OR

Educator: What would it take to move from a 4 to, say, a 6? What would a 6 be like? How much control do you have over running? How much do you want to move up?

Now the educator and the student have a means in place to discuss objectively something external—running—rather than having a battle of the wills. The teacher will be saved that phrase we all tire of using when we see students running in the halls: "Derek, walk please." The scale allows students to evaluate their own choices from now on: "Derek, where are you on your scale right now?"

Another example is a struggling student who, through use of the scale, shared that some days are 5s and some are 7s. The **plan** was to find out what made 7s and do more of it. Noticing what was different about the times when the student was at a 7 helped her focus on what worked and illustrated possible solutions.

A scale can be used for a quick solutioning. Ask a student to whom you've introduced the scale, as she or he walks in the door, "What's today going to be?" The student will say back a number. If it's fairly high, I'll respond with, "Cool," or, "I can't wait." If it's not too high, I'm very proactive and take a second to talk with the student about what she or he could do that might make it higher.

Scales are a solutioning technique that can be used in a variety of ways. They aid in externalizing the problem, establishing a **purpose** and discussing details of a **plan** (complete with a value) to achieve it, and then for monitoring **progress.** MASTER 30 "Language Lesson: Scaling" and MASTER 31 "Student Worksheet: Scaling Out a Plan" provide additional examples of uses of scales in solutioning and a step-by-step format for using them.

Scaling

MASTER 30

With a 10 being the best things could be and a 1 being the worst they could be, where are they right now? Where does the student want to be? Next week? What will that look like?

1	2	3	4	5	6	7	8	9	10
Worst									Best

You've turned in one assignment this week. Let's draw a scale and look at this. How do you want things to be? What number would that be? What would it take to move up one or two places? Where could you be by next week? How?

1	2	3	4	5	6	7	8	9	10
No assignments in									All assignments in

Scaling Steps

1. Ask the student to rate the current problem/situation. "Where are you now?"
2. Ask the student for a **purpose** value. "Where do you want to be?"
3. Ask for details of what would be different (behaviorally) at that value. "What would you be saying/doing/feeling/thinking differently at a(n) _____ ?"
4. Use the techniques in this chapter to firm up a **plan** to reach the desired value.
5. Continue to refer to the scale when discussing **progress** (Chapter 5).

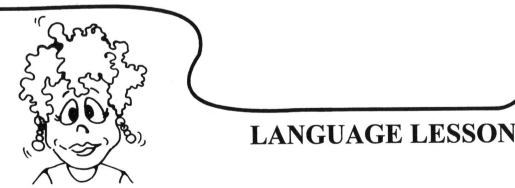

LANGUAGE LESSON

Scaling Out a Plan

MASTER 31

Name _____

Purpose: _____

Where are you on the scale right now?

_____

1	2	3	4	5	6	7	8	9	10
Worst									Best

Potentials: _____

_____

PLAN

Where do you want to be on the scale in _____ days? _____

1	2	3	4	5	6	7	8	9	10
Worst									Best

What will be different when you are at that number? _____

_____

What **potentials** are you going to use to get there? _____

_____

What is your **plan?** _____

_____

SOURCE: Adapted from *Solutioning: Solution-Focused Interventions for Counselors* (p. 158), by W. Webb, 1999, Philadelphia: Taylor and Francis/Accelerated Development. Used with permission.

One last hint. After students have shared **potentials,** made **plan** choices, and are ready to go, a statement can reinforce their creation of their own solutions—for example, "I am very proud of your coming up with this idea to stay out of fights. It fits you well," or, "You know, I agree with your **plan** to get to school on time. I know it will work," or "When you raise your grade, your parents may think I had something to do with it, but I think you should know that you deserve all the credit."

Chapter 4 Focused   *Lead students into effective **plans** with questioning rather than telling.*

Educator skills such as listening and creating achievable assignments are practiced daily in classrooms. These same skills are what help the solutioning team of educator and student create collaborative **plans** that result in change, problem resolution, and solutions (MASTER 32 "Educator Helpsheet: The Plan" and MASTER 33 "Student Worksheet: The Plan" are helpful summary forms). Using skills you already possess to lead students into effective **plans** only takes a little practice with questioning rather than telling. By using the Journey Through Solutioning Map (see Figure 4.1), the Language Lessons, and the other worksheets, **plans** will nearly form themselves. Don't be too shocked when students begin telling you what you were wanting to tell them all along and taking responsibility for doing it!

MASTER 32

POSITIVE:

Notice what works.
Observe for positives.
Take note of the things you want to continue or do more.

PRACTICE:

When you imagine yourself doing your solution, what will you be doing?

_____

_____

Don't do anything yet, just pretend yourself doing your **plan.**

PERFORM:

What exceptions/**potentials** from the past can you try again?

_____

_____

What current exceptions/**potentials** could you do more and in other areas?

_____

_____

Which of your *pretend potentials* could you begin doing now?

_____

_____

What ideas from other people can you begin trying?

_____

_____

The Plan

MASTER 33

Name _____ Date _____

The **purpose** of my **plan** is:

_____

The skills/abilities/**potentials** I have to do this **plan** are:

_____

_____

My **plan** is to:

_____

_____

The following will help me do my **plan**:

_____

_____

I will share this **plan** with:

_____

_____

I will discuss my **progress** on:

_____

_____

_____

5

Postcards Home
Progress

Progress may seem to come after some sort of solutioning conversation, intervention, or question has been used. With a solutioning focus, however, you will be using the skills of this chapter continually in many situations: prior to, during, and after a solutioning **plan** has been created (see Figure 5.1). Have you ever sent a postcard home? What did you emphasize? Most people share the positive. That is what the language of **progress** encourages students to do: find and share any and good results of their efforts, take responsibility for them, and use them further to create, finalize, or continue solutions.

Students are constantly growing, learning, and becoming, and we as educators are in there doing it with them. We must focus on the positive, growth, and process aspects in all of our conversations, thereby emphasizing the important life skills of continual self-improvement and learning while moving students toward a solutioning focus themselves. By using the language in this chapter, you will be discussing what students did to improve, make a difference, or keep things from getting worse while holding them accountable to their **plans** and adding consistency to the solutioning process (Webb, 1999). Look at the differences in following through on a **plan** in Chart 5.1. As a student, which would you prefer?

Nothing shows you care more than a positive follow-up question/response.

Practicing Responsible Success

After some **progress**, improvement, effort, or success has been made, attributing it appropriately is a valuable endeavor for responsibility, self-esteem, and enduring solutions. What good is change if it doesn't last? How many of you have experienced positive differences with students, just to find yourselves back in the same old rut again in no time? Falling back into old habits and patterns creates a great deal of frustration for students and burnout for educators. So,

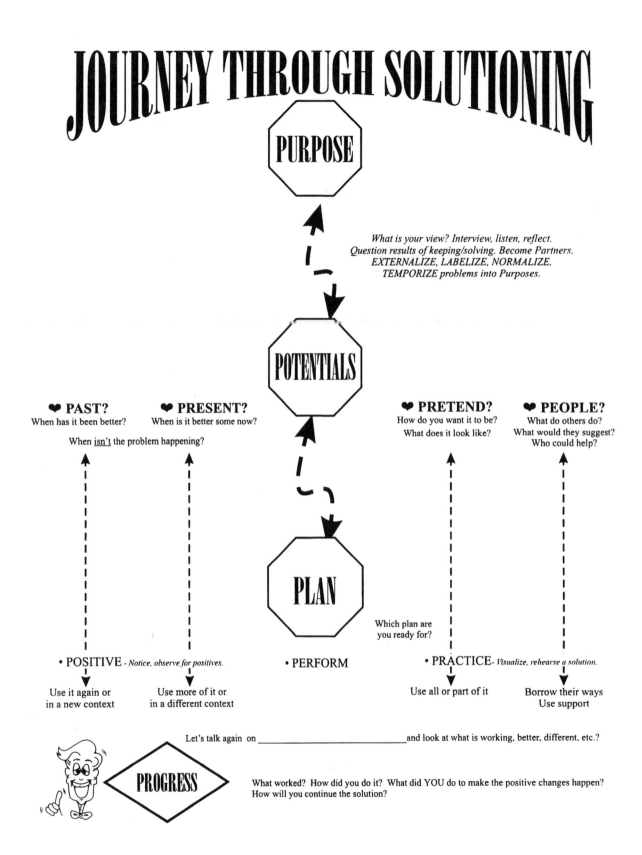

Figure 5.1. Journey Through Solutioning Map.

Willyn H. Webb, *The Educator's Guide to Solutioning.* Copyright © 1999 by Corwin Press, Inc.

Chart 5.1   Progress

Problem-Focused	Solutioning-Focused
"What went wrong?"	"What went right?"
"How do we fix/correct the shortcomings?"	"How do you do more of what worked?"
"Why was this the outcome?"	"What did you do to make a difference?"
"Good job."	"You (behavior). I'm impressed. How did you do that?"
Correct mistakes	Compliment effort, abilities, and any successes
Reprimand	Encourage
Punishment	Responsibility taking Real consequences
New **plan**	Build on what worked
Disappointment, frustration, or empty praise, cheerleading	Joint acknowledgement of what parts were better
	Earned self-esteem
Follow-up forgotten	**Progress** celebrated, process ongoing
Causes, past	Solutions, future

let's empower students to practice responsible success through the language of **progress** designed to do three things:

1. Increase students' ownership of solutions-responsible success

2. Build students' self-esteem

3. Make lasting change a reality

Nothing shows you care more than a positive follow-up question/response. Look through MASTER 34 "Language Lesson: Practicing Responsible Success." Can you begin using some of those ideas now? Perhaps after assignments? When something good happens? After solutioning? Help students own and take responsibility for any **progress,** any positives, and most of all, any success.

Practicing Responsible Success

MASTER 34

After a *Positive Plan*

What did you find _____ (e.g., in your life, about school, about math, at recess) that you like, that is positive, that works?

What good things did your detective work unveil?

Tell me about your observations of the positive.

After a *Practice Plan*

How did your practice go?

What benefits did you gain from visualizing your solution?

Is your solution ready to go?

Tell me about how your *practice plan* happened.

What parts of your visualization got easier, happened?

After a *Perform Plan*

What about your solution/**plan** worked, helped, went well?

Tell me about the difference your **plan** made.

Tell me about how your solution was successful.

What parts of the **plan** helped the most, worked the best?

What did *you* do new or differently that made a change, a difference, or helped?

When did you feel better, more confident, on the ball?

What feelings did you have that you like?

During what part of the day do you feel the best?

Are there times when you would have expected to feel _____ but you didn't?

What positive thoughts did you have?

When were you thinking clearly?

LANGUAGE LESSON

Practicing Responsible Success

MASTER 34 Continued

What good decisions did you make?

What thoughts were in mind when _____ (e.g., you were feeling better, you were on-track)?

What messages did you give yourself about your solution?

What did you say to yourself that worked, helped?

When did you get along with others this week?

Whom were you with when things were better?

Which people help you? Whom are you with when you're feeling better/good/using a solution?

What positive interactions did you have?

Who else noticed when your solution was successful?

SOURCE: Adapted from *Solutioning: Solution-Focused Interventions for Counselors* (pp. 170-173), by W. Webb, 1999, Philadelphia: Taylor and Francis/Accelerated Development. Used with permission.

Feedback

You really made that happen.

It sounds as if you made a change in the right direction.

You did (positive change), and (positive result) happened.

When you (thought, feeling, behavior), that really made a difference.

Sounds to me as if you made some great things happen in your life.

Wow, you really took control.

It seems as if things are better because of what you've done.

Follow through with:

How did you do that?

Add your own here:

LANGUAGE LESSON

Self-Esteem the Old-Fashioned Way

The emphasis on the "How did you do that?" question empowers students with expert status over their own solutions, positive behaviors, and abilities. If we remain expert over them, then they will be dependent on us for their self-esteem. Getting self-esteem from others doesn't work. Notice how the language of solutioning sets up students to realize, own, and appreciate their own accomplishments. Through the focus and process, students will be able to get self-esteem the old-fashioned way—earn it for themselves.

You'll be surprised. Students are rarely aware of the solutions they use and the skills they possess. It is our job to help students fully acknowledge their competencies and abilities. By taking responsibility for solutions, students not only earn self-esteem but also own a skill they can use again. This makes solutions last. Dana Huskey found this with her 4-year-old son.

Chill Out

Journal entry of Dana Huskey (Used with permission from Dana Huskey)

Sunday evening, while coming home from church, I commented on how I had noticed how quiet my son had been in church. I asked him how he had done that. He said, "I guess I 'chilled out.' "

This child had a name for a skill/solution that Dana and many other parents have struggled to teach. Dana commented in my adult class that he was very proud of himself when he had the chance to share his skill. She believes that, without the observing and questioning skills of solutioning, the exception to the rule (being quiet) would have gone unacknowledged and the skill missed. The old pattern of noise in church would have been a likely result. As it turned out, her son continued to be quiet with a quick reminder of, "Remember, when you are chilling out, church is OK."

Over the years, countless self-esteem curricula have come and gone. Despite our efforts, many students still seem to have low opinions of themselves, as demonstrated by the prevalence of drugs, alcohol, promiscuity, and violence plaguing our teens. The solutioning focus believes that educators cannot give students the internal belief in themselves that leads to responsibility with extrinsic rewards, empty praise, or curriculum. It has to be earned. Hwang (1995) points out, "Too often, self-esteem programs send completely counterproductive messages to children by directing youngsters' attention toward their own basest inner gratification—no matter what you do, it's fine, because you are always wonderful and special" (p. 488). Setting **purposes,** looking at **potentials,** finding solutions, and carrying out **plans** empower students toward self-worth. The **progress** language of solutioning emphasizes students realizing for themselves the behavior they did to make a positive difference; it was not just our cheering them on. Laura Schlessinger (1994) believes that "[t]he quality of our lives ultimately depends on the courage we extend to deal with hurt and risk in a creative way: That is the road to ever growing self-esteem. And those challenges are available at every age" (p. 41). Solutioning provides this type of challenge by not telling students what to do, by not solving their problems for them, and most important, by handling **progress** in a manner that sets up students to find their own successes and take responsibility for them.

Additionally, assisting students in pretending and then realizing desired tomorrows builds the character and self-esteem they will need throughout their lives. "Because if you can dream for your future, it means you believe in yourself now" (Schlessinger, 1994, p. 85). Let's equip students with the confidence and ability to dream so that drug dealers, self-pleasing thrill seekers, or gangs are not such powerful influences anymore.

Progress *notes encourage students to reflect on their behavior, take responsibility for it, and earn self-esteem.*	**Written in Stone**

For many students, especially those with low self-esteem, seeing is believing. Write down what **progress** you see and question students so that they, too, acknowledge their competency. Have students write down what worked (as in MASTER 41 "Student Worksheet: Progress") and pour the solution cement. Jo Johnston, a master educator, used solutioning very cleverly to empower her student to acknowledge his own solutions.

Monty

Journal entry of Jo Johnston, middle-level teacher (Used with permission from Jo Johnston)

Monty is a sixth-grader. His dress is gang culture, and he is allowed to wear a baseball cap in school because of scars on his scalp. He always wears his cap. He looks at me with half-closed eyes, which are just barely visible beneath his cap. He mumbles when he talks, and I almost always ask him to repeat what he says. He gives the impression of being slow, but his previous teachers say he is very capable. He changed his last name on the first day of school so that he would be next to his friends alphabetically in physical education. During one testing period, he hit another student with a ruler and grabbed a girl around the waist and tried to wrestle her to the mat. I sent him to Think Tank. He refused to go. I threatened to call the assistant principal and suggested that he not make the situation worse. He tore the pass out of my hand and shouted that he would tell his mother. Monty was later suspended for an accumulation of Think Tank referrals.

After choosing him for the solutioning class, I noticed these positive attributes from the past: He reads and writes on grade level and can be a leader. I have noticed these positive attributes in the present: He stays on-task, gets along with peers better lately, and has a happier facial expression (after a few solutioning conversations). Tomorrow, I will give him the following note:

Monty, I would like your help with a student who isn't doing too well at Columbine. Would you be willing to write on a sheet of paper one or two things that have helped you? I won't use your name when I talk to this student. I hope you can help.

Thanks, Ms. Johnston

I asked the secretary to deliver the note to Monty in the morning before he came to my class. I included a blank sheet of paper with the note. I found the following reply on the paper, lying on my grade book when I came up from the locker room.

I try to pay better attention to what the teacher is saying and if I know what I'm doing wrong I try to talk to myself to stop myself before I do something that gets me in trouble.

Mrs. Johnston I hope this helps.
(he signed his first and last name)

Ms. Johnston blended many solutioning ideas (other frame of reference, focus on what does work, positive assumption) to encourage Monty to realize his own **progress.** Can you ever imagine getting a response like that from lecture, discipline, or traditional problem solving? The focus and the language are powerful. This student just acknowledged his own self-worth and, more important, specific behaviors he can continue to use.

Pointing out exceptions/**potentials** can come after some **progress** has been made or after the exploration of **potentials** to further highlight the solution and encourage the **plan.** Using the language you have been learning, write the note to fit the situation and the student. Yes, we all have too much paperwork as it is, but this is one piece of paper with a direct payoff. The results/solutions/positive behaviors may last the entire year.

MASTER 35 "Language Lesson: Written Progress" gives some tips for writing **progress**-type notes to students, encouraging them to reflect on their behavior, take responsibility for it, and earn self-esteem. Adapt, as did Jo Johnston, blending in various aspects of solutioning. Remember, you may or may not get answers to the "How did you do that?"-type questions, but the students are pondering it, and that makes an incredible difference.

Written Progress

MASTER 35

Begin with something you are impressed with—a strength, a coping skill, a **potential** (e.g., this may have been noticed, discovered during questioning, or a part of the **plan** that worked).

When appropriate, tie it to the **purpose, plan,** and so on.

End with a sentence that is hopeful, empowering, and motivating and that will encourage continuation.

Don't send too many or too often; they may lose their value.

Make the note personal and spontaneous, not formal and calculated.

Use language that assumes the positive change will continue to happen and the student will make the difference.

Short and simple is usually most effective.

Handwritten notes are more personal.

> (student's name),
> I am so impressed with (**potential** highlighted during solutioning or noticed). It seems things are better (or state **purpose**) when you (**potential** solution). I can't wait for you to tell me all about it when you are (**plan**).
> signed, (educator's name)

> (student's name),
> I am really impressed with your ability to _____ (e.g., be on time, turn in work, get along, talk nicely). How did (do) you do it? I bet you are sure glad to know that you have that _____ (e.g., skill, solution, answer). Just wanted to let you know I _____ (e.g., noticed, am proud, think it's cool).
> signed, (educator's name)

SOURCE: Adapted from *Solutioning: Solution-Focused Interventions for Counselors* (p. 216), by W. Webb, 1999, Philadelphia: Taylor and Francis/Accelerated Development. Used with permission.

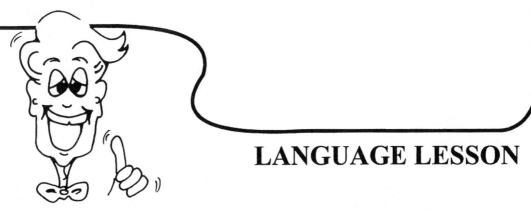

LANGUAGE LESSON

Solution Statements   *Solutioning is not solely a questioning technique;*
                                 the idea is to highlight recent changing.

Questions have been the emphasis of solutioning so far. Solutioning is not solely a questioning technique, however. A solution statement reflects back to students what we already see that is working, the best **potentials** they have shared, and/or **progress** we have seen them make. The idea is to highlight recent changing, an application of positive reinforcement, which we were all drilled on in our education programs and have experienced as valuable in our classrooms and families (Walter & Peller, 1992). Generally, students really enjoy being told what they are doing right, especially in a situation where they thought they might be "in trouble." With some students, it may be difficult to find material; however, being solutioning focused is *always* finding something positive to acknowledge, especially during follow-up or **progress.**

I'm Impressed . . .

Sally's parents were so critical of her that she thought she couldn't win for losing, so to speak. The parents came to conferences, mostly complaining about their daughter. They mentioned between critical remarks, however, that they had recently changed their routines to try to help their "helpless" daughter. This was followed by more griping about her lack of success despite their recent efforts. I was tempted to defend Sally and to share some of the talents I knew she possessed. This would have just put us at odds. Instead, I made a solution statement about their willingness to be available. "I am impressed with the willingness of both of you to make yourselves available to help your daughter. Mom, your persistence at being there to greet her and ask how her day was every day after school is commendable. Dad, your nightly study sessions with Sally after a busy day really show how much you care." These were positive things the parents were doing and were a great start on our forward journey toward sharing some positives of Sally.

Solution statements are beyond cheerleading. Students have responded with such awe-inspired comments as, "Wow, I didn't know I could do that," and, "No way, you mean I am already solving this problem?" Not all positive comments are helpful, however. According to Deci and Flaste (1995), the difference between encouraging and discouraging praise lies in whether its origin is in controlling or noncontrolling. Solution statements are not designed to manipulate or control students, but rather to assist them in realizing and using their own **potentials** and **progress.** The difference lies in who is made the authority, who is given credit (or not), and whether it is followed through with a responsibility-giving question. Do you try to *give* students answers through praise? "Class, thanks for your quiet entry," or, "You all brought your books, so now you can have 5 minutes free time at the end," or, "Good job, much better than yesterday. Now you'll get the reward," compared with, "You came in quietly. How did you manage to control wanting to talk so well?" or, "Everyone brought his or her books. How did you all concentrate that much?" or, "Good job. How did you turn yourself around like that?"

A simple statement like, "I'm amazed. You've been handling this situation really well. How are you doing it?" though not specific, can be very helpful in changing students' views of themselves—from victims to coping. Waiting until the **plan** stage or until some **progress** has been made seems to have a greater impact than "Good job" or "That's great" as you go along. By waiting, you have the full attention of the student who has, until now, mostly been answering questions. Now it is the educator's turn to respond, and to respond strongly with a solution statement. Remember, "The intentions of the praiser do not matter. What matters is how the child feels as a result of the praise" (Gootman, 1997, p. 47).

Let's Talk

Journal entry of Sandi Kropeunske, high school science teacher (Used with permission from Sandi Kropeunske)

We ended up in a family discussion about cars. My husband started to give [our daughter] advice. I added my confidence in her ability from the past week's incident. Almost instantly, she became more talkative and open to discuss more during our conversation, rather than her normal way of shutting us out. It was great!

See what you can sincerely mean and comment on with students by using MASTER 36 "Language Lesson: Solution Statements" and MASTER 37 "Practice Makes Perfect: Solution Statements."

Solution Statements

MASTER 36

1. Be genuine.
2. Mention a behavior, skill, exception, achievement, and so on.
3. Share the authority whenever possible with a question such as "How did you do that?"
4. Use sparingly to get the most value.
5. Emphasize efforts.

Example Situation: Alicia is a high school student with no self-confidence. You often overhear her bragging about boys using her and about her wild weekend escapades. She reminds you of a stray dog that craves attention. She is failing a few classes and may not graduate. Her **purpose** for solutioning is to figure out a way to graduate. During a discussion of *past potentials,* she shares that she liked elementary school and "did pretty good then." Alicia shares during *pretend potentials* that she is good at always dressing in the latest trends. She likes to keep up on the world of fashion.

Example Solution Statement: "Alicia, I am impressed with the way you keep up on the fashion world. How do you do that, keep up so well?" (Now she can elaborate on this skill and then apply it to her schoolwork.) You could follow with a question about whether/how she kept up in grade school and acknowledge that as well. This brings out a skill she may not realize she has that can be applied as her solution.

Example Situation: D'André had a **plan** to put all of his materials in his folder when he got to school each morning and then carry it with him all day, thus having his materials for each class. He had tried it for 3 days and had made it to most of his classes with paper and pencil.

Example Solution Statement: "D'André, you've had materials in most of your classes. How have you managed to be so organized for the past 3 days? What about your **plan** to use the folder worked the best?" Now, D'André can elaborate on the part that worked best and apply it more or to the classes in which he still forgets. This is very different from a discussion of why he couldn't get materials to all classes and what went wrong in the ones he didn't.

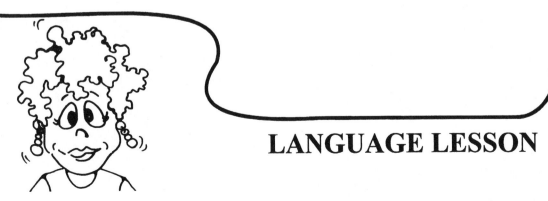

LANGUAGE LESSON

Practice Makes Perfect
SOLUTION STATEMENTS

MASTER 37

Situation #1: Paddy is a third-grader who gets in fights weekly. He seems to have a chip on his shoulder. The **purpose** he had for solutioning was to not have detention anymore and to get to go to computers on Friday. He acknowledges that getting along (positive representation) is the way to do this. The **potentials** he shares are getting along with two brothers and two sisters at home most of the time and being able to calm down when he thinks of how mad Dad will be. He has just completed 1 full day without a fight.

Solution Statement:

_____

_____

_____

_____

Situation #2: Chance is seventh-grader. He is the class clown and a skilled cheater. He has been caught twice, however, and received zeros. The **purpose** he has for solutioning is to pass a test on his own so that he doesn't get a zero again. During **potentials,** he shares that he can remember many answers by just glancing at another student's test just once or twice. This is clarified as good memorization skills. He has just received a D on a test (on his own).

Solution Statement:

_____

_____

_____

_____

(continued)

Practice Makes Perfect

SOLUTION STATEMENTS

MASTER 37 Continued

Situation #3: April has not turned in any assignments with her name on them. She is consistent at forgetting. Her **purpose** for solutioning is to remember her name so that she gets credit for her work. The externalized problem is forgetting. During **potentials,** she shares that she always remembers to get the mail at home. You share that she has never forgotten her lunch ticket. She also says she always knows the answers to the problems.

Solution Statement:

_____

_____

_____

_____

Situation #4: Athena has done great work in your class except that whenever she is absent, she does no makeup work. This has brought down Athena's grade. Her **purpose** for solutioning is to do the makeup work for an upcoming 3-day absence. The **potentials** shared are (a) doing well on regular assignments and (b) doing some makeup work last year before she got so busy. Some, but not all, of the makeup work was turned in.

Solution Statement:

_____

_____

_____

_____

Once you have a positive skill, a solution, use it for all it's worth.   **Lasting Change**

Stopping with responsibility and pride in successfully solving a problem, using a skill, or developing a competency is of little use if old, negative patterns, behaviors, or problems return. Nothing is more frustrating than dealing with the same students with the same difficulties over and over. The solutioning process itself encourages permanence of solutions (student-discovered, -chosen, and -owned); however, discussing continuation during the celebration of **progress** may be helpful. Once you have a positive skill, a solution, use it for all it's worth.

Maude

Journal entry of Wayne Crick, middle-level science teacher (Used with permission from Wayne Crick)

I had a piece of paper with several questions on it for Maude at the end of class. The questions were "When you were behaving properly just a few days ago, what was class like?" "As a student who behaves properly, do you feel any negative vibes from the instruction?" "What are the classroom expectations for all students pertaining to talking out of turn?" and "I really liked it when you were not talking and being disruptive. What are your thoughts on what you had to do to make your behavior so positive, and how will you continue them?" Maude began to act positively more often than talk, which was still very tempting for her. These questions were never actually discussed, just reflected on, and through them I expressed my faith in her, something the other methods I had used did not allow me to do. Once I had a good day from her, I knew I must do what I could, positively, to keep it going. This was so much more pleasant and effective than the verbal reprimands, time-in after class, and so on.

This case study shows (a) the value in making students experts over their behavior and responsible for their accomplishments so that they can be continued and (b) how the language of solutioning can be easily blended into your own style. Mr. Crick adapted his words and style of communicating through notes while still expressing the same assumptions and questioning for responsibility, which empowered Maude to take control and continue proper behavior.

Project **progress** into the future with one more question/statement. Use MASTER 38 "Language Lesson: Lasting Change" for ideas.

It is entirely worth it to carry out a meaningful follow-up with a student if that keeps things moving ahead. It saves time in the long run. (Chris Ames, middle-level language arts teacher)

Lasting Change

MASTER 38

How will you keep these positive changes going?

How are you going to continue this happening?

What can you do so that this happens even more?

How can you encourage the change to continue, increase, last?

Who can help you keep this positive **progress** happening?

Name all of the things you did that you can continue.

What will ensure that the difference you are seeing now will continue?

What can you do tomorrow to help things stay on-track?

What parts of the **plan** are you going to keep doing?

Feedback

Now that you know what works, you can do it more/again.

I am so impressed that you've figured out something that makes things better (be specific) so that you can look forward to school now.

It sounds to me as if you have what you need to continue feeling/thinking/acting so great.

You seem to feel proud of the changes you have made and ready to keep it up.

Experimenting, Contests, Games

Let's experiment with this new skill and see whether you can do it for another week.

Let's see who can continue to _____ (e.g., say the most nice things, do the most around the house, turn in the most homework).

How about making a game out of it? Each time you feel like cheating, sharpen your pencil first.

This is working great. Let's have a stress-free contest.

Scaling, Percentages, and Ratings

Where would you rate your **progress** on a scale of 1 to 10, 1 being the worst and 10 being the best? How can you continue moving up? What did you do to keep from going down farther that you can use now to move up?

How many notches have you moved up? How did you do that? How many do you want to move up now? How might you do it?

How would you rate this week, compared with last week? Where do you want to be by the end of next week?

Add your own:

SOURCE: Adapted from *Solutioning: Solution-Focused Interventions for Counselors* (pp. 211, 213), by W. Webb, 1999, Philadelphia: Taylor and Francis/Accelerated Development. Used with permission.

LANGUAGE LESSON

The solutioning process itself mirrors the structure of a story.   **Solutioning Stories**

Successful solutioning can be compared to a new story/movie for the future. White and Epston (1990) have done extensive writings and work with narrative:

> If we accept that persons organize and give meaning to their experience through the storying of experience, and that in the performance of these stories they express selected aspects of their lived experience, then it follows that these stories are constitutive—shaping lives and relationships. (p. 12)

Many of us, adults and students alike, tell the stories of our problems, the calamities, the trials and tribulations, so to speak, to anyone who will listen. We are less likely to tell stories of successes, triumphs, and victories. Would this be unacceptable, inappropriate, or labeled bragging? During a look at **progress,** assist students in storying their success, thus making it part of their life scripts, taking credit, and owning it for the future. Throughout the 3-P process, students have already been "reauthoring" by forming new, more useful perceptions (White & Epston, 1990). The solutioning process itself mirrors the structure of a story, as shown below:

Story Structure	*Solutioning Process*
1. Introduction	1. Open conversation
2. Problem	2. **Purpose**
3. Event sequence	3. **Potentials**
4. Resolution (problem solution)	4. **Plan**
5. Conclusion	5. **Progress**

SOURCE: Adapted from *Solutioning: Solution-Focused Interventions for Counselors* (p. 256), by W. Webb, 1999, Philadelphia: Taylor and Francis/Accelerated Development. Used with permission.

Carol the Smiler

As shared by a workshop participant

Carol was in my fourth-grade class. She walked to school and was frequently late. This was not her biggest problem, however. Carol would come to school in a "mood," either good or bad, and the rest of her day would follow suit. We never could get a feel for what was happening at home or on the way that would result in either mood, so when I learned about solutioning and the emphasis on solutions rather than causes, I thought it would be perfect for Carol. Soon after I attended a solutioning workshop, Carol came to class on time and in a great mood. This was my opportunity, and I wanted to use it to encourage permanent change. Carol loved stories and was a very dramatic storyteller herself. I chose a solutioning story question to ask Carol when I greeted her.

Educator: Carol, you are having a great day. If I would have spied on you this morning, what would I have seen that made you in such a great mood and on time? Tell me the story of you coming to school.

Carol: You would have seen me wake up grumpy and yelling back and forth with my mom. Then on the way to school you would have seen me decide to change feeling bad to feeling good and put a smile on my face.

Educator: So, when you put a smile on your face as you're walking to school, you can have a great day. I am so glad to know that. I bet you are too.

Carol: Yeah, I was a little surprised at how well it worked. I think I'll try it tomorrow too.

Educator: I like that idea. I'll look forward to another great day tomorrow.

Carol came to school more consistently on time and in better moods—not all the time, but the difference was powerful. I never knew what happened at home, but I worried less about it, knowing that Carol could turn things around by putting on a smile. Her self-control increased tremendously. I wonder whether she would have made "putting on a smile" part of her new life story without the questions of solutioning. With a simple acknowledgement, praise, or reward for the good day, she may not have reauthored her story and realized her new skill.

Regardless of the amount of **progress** made, we need to help students give their stories a positive slant to motivate further efforts. Metcalf (1995) suggests questions as ways to gather information about how the student perceives his or her story and assist in reauthoring. These and useful others are found in MASTER 39 "Language Lesson: Solution Stories." MASTER 40 "Once Upon a Time . . ." follows. It may be given to older students, done together, or used as a guide for a solutioning story conversation.

Solution Stories

MASTER 39

If I were a fly on the wall, what would I see you doing in your classroom that would tell me things had changed for you?

Describe the video game (movie, story) of your life from now on. Tell how you win over the problem, how other characters react, and the successes.

If I asked Jing-wei, your best friend, how she saw you acting differently during choir so that you didn't get points taken off, what would she say?

After you have raised your grade to a C, what's the first privilege you will ask your parents to give back? The second?

Like a real scientist, report for me the results of your experiment with winning over _____ (e.g., laziness, anger, boredom).

Pretend this is a game show and you are in a contest against ditching. Be the game show host and tell me who wins and how. Don't forget the prizes (benefits).

When you are no longer in trouble in class, what do you think you'll be able to do that you haven't been able to do for a while? Tell it like a movie, story, or play.

Now that you have completed a week of all smiley faces and can go to computers on Friday, what is the first computer game you are going to play? How will you do it next week? Tell me that story.

If I followed you around tomorrow (or next week) when things are different, what behaviors would you point out and describe to me as different?

If I were to spy on you tomorrow morning as you get ready for school, what would I see you doing, exactly, that would help you turn in your homework when you get here?

Add your own here:

SOURCE: Adapted from *Solutioning: Solution-Focused Interventions for Counselors* (p. 258), by W. Webb, 1999, Philadelphia: Taylor and Francis/Accelerated Development. Used with permission.

LANGUAGE LESSON

MASTER 40

Once Upon a Time . . .

Introduction: (open conversation, share worldview, listen)

Let's talk about _____. What would you like to share?

_____

_____

Problem: (define, clarify, externalize, establish a **purpose**)

What are your concerns? How do you want things to be?

_____

_____

Event Sequence: (question about exceptions to the problem and **potential** solutions—*past, present, pretend, people*)
When have things been better? When do things work now? How do you imagine your problem being solved? What ideas can you get from others? Who could help?

_____

_____

_____

Resolution: (choose a **potential,** make a **plan,** and solve the problem)

_____

_____

_____

Conclusion: (talk again to celebrate what worked)

_____

_____

_____

SOURCE: Adapted from *Solutioning: Solution-Focused Interventions for Counselors* (pp. 259-260), by W. Webb, 1999, Philadelphia: Taylor and Francis/Accelerated Development. Used with permission.

Solutioning progress is not based on treats, rewards, awards, or praises, but on realization, responsibility, and continued momentum.

Chapter 5 Focused

Solutioning payoffs are the solutions themselves, the feelings of self-worth, the pride in efforts, and the internal satisfaction. With the solutioning focus of concentrating on what works, **progress** and motivation are ongoing. Empower students with life skills like independence, awareness of abilities, responsibility, and intrinsic motivation with a simple, well-worded question/statement, rather than with a candy bar that is quickly digested and forgotten.

MASTER 41

Things I did (solutions) that worked (describe in detail):

_____

_____

_____

How I did it:

_____

_____

_____

Things others (e.g., teacher, friends, parents) noticed I did that worked:

_____

_____

_____

Things (solutions) I can do again, more, a lot:

_____

_____

_____

How I can do it again, more, a lot. My plan:

_____

_____

_____

6

Why Stop Now?

Solutioning Discipline, Classroom Management, and Lessons

Why wait until a problem arises or use the solutioning focus only for interactions? Why stop now? The solutioning focus is applicable to most areas of school and classroom life. What do you do for discipline? Classroom management? Instruction? Assessment? Where could you apply the solutioning focus? Actualize the utility and value of solutioning by incorporating it into all aspects of your role in education. The benefits for you and your students will be high self-esteem, self-control, responsibility, enjoyment, learning, and growth.

According to Gallup polls, discipline is of utmost concern to educators and is viewed by the American public as a major problem in education (Elam et al., 1994; Elam & Rose, 1995; Gallup, 1994; Rose, Gallup, & Elam, 1997). According to Smith and Riveria (1995), "Many reasons are cited for the lack of discipline in school settings: for example, low teacher salaries, insufficient funding for education, lack of parental support, and a disregard for authority by students" (p. 1). Sounds like the teacher's lounge to me. How much impact can one really have on changing the above-named causes enough to make a difference? So why waste time with why?

> Many of these problems are beyond the control of educators, but must not be used as an excuse for why discipline problems cannot be ameliorated. Rather, educators must focus on identifying and addressing the individual needs of students, improving the educational environment, using effective prevention and intervention techniques, and building collaborative partnerships. (p. 1)

Discipline, Classroom Management, and Solutioning

Sounds as if they are describing solutioning's application to discipline and classroom management. If you are looking to build a case for why students are out of control in your classroom, you will find plenty of excuses but make little difference. If you are looking to build on individual abilities, on your own strengths, on the positive aspects of your school system, on teaming up with students, parents, and administration, and on a positive, effective learning environment, you will make a real difference.

Although not designed specifically as a "discipline program," the focus and language of solutioning serve many disciplinary needs. Solutioning offers a refreshing alternative to "quick fix" programs that leave you dealing with the same problems over and over and/or programs so all-encompassing that you have to change everything you do to incorporate them. Solutioning is easily blended in with existing programs and school policies by altering just slightly the language you use when interacting with students.

From a solutioning focus, discipline should help students develop self-control, responsibility, and life skills, rather than force external control on them. When problems (inevitable when working with human beings) do arise, solutioning provides a nonaccusatory method of intervention that offers individualized consistency. A solutioning educator sees students as capable and is willing to give students the choice and responsibility that lead to a safe, disciplined learning environment. Notice the differences in Chart 6.1.

How do you view/use discipline—to control? to teach? Brewer, Dunn, and Olszewski (1988) refer to the importance of the control decision:

> [A] given teacher approaches classroom management from one of two primary conceptual stances: (1) the control inherent in classroom management resides in the teachers and is characterized by external motivation, including the administration or withholding of rewards, or (2) the control inherent in class management resides in individual students. (p. 152)

This basic question of whether we need to control our students or to set them up to control themselves is one rarely asked. None of my adult students have yet to share that a college preparation course helped them make such a decision. Yet, a common experience of educators, even master teachers, is struggling with encouraging responsibility while maintaining order. All educators want to encourage student responsibility, but many don't have the tools and are afraid of losing control, which is where solutioning is so beneficial.

Solutioning provides the language to achieve student responsibility and self-control. As Lincoln (1993) points out, "You can't teach self-discipline part of the day, then at other times take an authoritarian or permissive stance" (p. 38). The solutioning focus sets the preventive stage for the 3-P process to flourish when intervention is necessary. The consistency is not only individualized but also inherent in the language. "Prevention techniques establish the foundation on which teachers can implement additional interventions and promote a positive classroom environment" (Smith & Riveria, 1995, p. 3).

Chart 6.1   Discipline

Problem-Focused, Traditional	Solutioning-Focused
External, authority control	Self-control
Rules	Procedures
Punishments, rewards	Self-control
Educator enforces what NOT to do	Educator teaches what TO DO
Quick fixes	Permanent solutions
Consequences are "one size fits all"	Individualized consistency
Power struggles	Cooperation
Reactionary	Preventive
Harsh, punitive	Caring, encouraging
Doing to students	Interacting with students
Built on power	Built on trust/communication
Hassle	Learning opportunity
Fear	Motivation
Adversaries	Partners
"I have strict rules so that my students won't walk all over me."	"What kind of classroom do we want to have?"
"This is my room, and I'm in charge."	"We all learn here, and procedures help things go smoothly."
"I don't like to rule my students to death."	"Expectations and procedures teach students what to do."
"These students have no respect, and I have to do what it takes to keep them under control."	"I respect them, and they respect me."

Freed from much of the burden of controlling students, solutioning educators can spend more time on enhancing learning. According to Gootman (1997), "[A]s children learn how to take responsibility for their own behavior, teachers find that the time they must spend on discipline problems diminishes" (p. 3). The benefits of empowering students with self-control are immense: "People with a strong sense of ownership and control (i.e., people who believe they can make things happen) are more motivated to learn than those who feel they lack control" (Furtwengler, 1996, pp. 36-37).

In this Postmodern Day world where we teach, the "controlling teacher" has no place. Students are more independent, wiser, and less conforming. They want to take more responsibility. Solutioning provides a "solution" for educators in meeting the needs of these students. (Elaine Robey, Occoquan Elementary School, Woodbridge, VA)

Being proactive, forward moving, and solutioning focused is much more productive than trying to figure out why students behave the way they do, why the old techniques don't work anymore, and why they can't be controlled. The solutioning focus highlights when students are behaving correctly, positively, and learning, rather than when they are not. This is not a denial of the infractions (that is when you intervene with the 3-P process), but an emphasis on the opposite. This is the idea of "you get what you look for, notice, and acknowledge" applied to discipline.

> Quite simply, if we notice our kids when they're misbehaving or being irresponsible, or we constantly say, "Don't touch that" or "Don't be a bad boy," that's what we'll get more of. But if we notice and acknowledge when they're being responsible or behaving well, we'll get more of that. (Vannoy, 1994, p. 62)

Noticing students behaving appropriately and focusing on solutions will create a classroom/school where this is what happens the majority of the time. It is so simple and so easy, yet so rare, as we go out to lunch duty and monitor for rule breakers, stand in the halls and yell at students who are running, and send students to the office for wrongdoings. Imagine the opposite—standing in the lunchroom noticing good manners and polite conversation; pointing out students who are walking in the halls; or sending students to the principal for doing something exceptional. If you are thinking that behind your back other students are throwing food, writing on walls, or laughing at you, you're wrong. In actuality, you will get more good manners, more walking, and more exceptional behavior. Try it and see.

When problems arise, which is inevitable, solutioning provides individualized consistency. As Gootman (1997) points out, "Students and circumstances differ. In my opinion, consequences should not be 'one size fits all'" (p. 41). Of course, going through the 3-P process is not an option with every infraction. Asking students, "What could you be doing instead?" is just as quick as saying, "Sit down and get to work." The difference in the amount of respect and responsibility, however, is tremendous. "Emphasizing technique is a narrow solution for student discipline" (Short & Short, 1992, p. 567). Solutioning is beyond technique; it is a process that consistently individualizes for students; teaches them a skill; encourages self-control, self-regulation, and thinking; and provides forward-moving interaction. Put the solutioning focus into action with positive expectations (a **purpose**), clear procedures (the **potentials**), organized objectives and effective instructional methods (a **plan**) following through with balanced assessment, and immediate and effective feedback (**progress**). Within this type of structure are safety and stability because students can depend on educators' consistency. Within this type of structure, self-control and responsibility flourish.

Expectations = Purpose

A solutioning focus on expectations sets up a climate where student input is encouraged and valued. Appropriate for both educators and students, the **potentials** question "How do you want things to be?" leads directly into student/educator expectations for themselves, their school, their classroom, and their learning. Very responsible. Promote a positive learning climate where interactions are valued and outbursts are rare with a joint **purpose.**

> Working with students to build a safe, caring community takes time, patience, and skill. It's no surprise, then, that discipline programs fall back on what's easy: punishments ("consequences") and re- wards . . . In a consequence-based classroom, students are led to ask, "What does she want me to do, and what happens to me if I don't do it?" In a reward-based classroom, they're led to ask, "What does she want me to do, and what do I get for doing it?" And notice how different either one is from what we'd like children to think about: "What kind of person do I want to be?" or "What kind of classroom do we want to have?" (Kohn, 1995, p. 34)

Silence

Journal entry of Wayne Crick, middle-level science teacher (Used with permission from Wayne Crick)

The class had been exhibiting more unacceptable behavior lately that needed to be adjusted. When I entered the classroom after hall duty for the next 2 days, I asked, "How do you want things to be?" and, "What would the classroom be like when the instructor entered the room and it was quiet?" There was a silence in the room as students thought. I followed with, "Who would be the first to notice the room was quiet?" My next question was, "Can you imagine what the room would sound like?" I left them to reflect on that and, enjoying the quiet, began the lesson. Of course, when I walked in the next day and the room was silent, I made sure I noticed and followed with the **progress** questions. This took care of the problem, and I didn't have any new rules, there were no lectures, no reprimands, and no punishments!

By having your own positive **purpose,** you will create self-fulfilling prophecies. Step into your classroom, believing that students will learn and grow. This belief will come across to them and it will happen. Compare this with stepping into your classroom, believing that students will be problems and must be shut down or controlled. Of course, just expecting the positive and focusing on what works are not magic and not enough. The natural mistakes of learning and the limit testing of growing up are inevitable. Gootman (1997) points out, "Just expecting the positive is not enough; however, it starts us off on the right foot" (p. 34).

By using solutioning and encouraging students to establish their own positive **purposes,** you are starting them out on the right foot. As Chris Ames pointed out in her journal,

Maybe a simple vision, combining mine with theirs, would be a good direction to move. We all want the best possible class. (Christine Ames, middle-level language arts teacher; used with permission from Christine Ames)

A valuable topic for discussing or writing on the first day of school (and much more fun that having rules read over and over) can be around the very simple question "How do you want things to be?" Revisiting this topic throughout the year instills ownership, control, and responsibility within students. Begin with the reflection questions on MASTER 42 "Reflection: Expectations = Purpose." These will prepare you and lead into a valuable discussion with students.

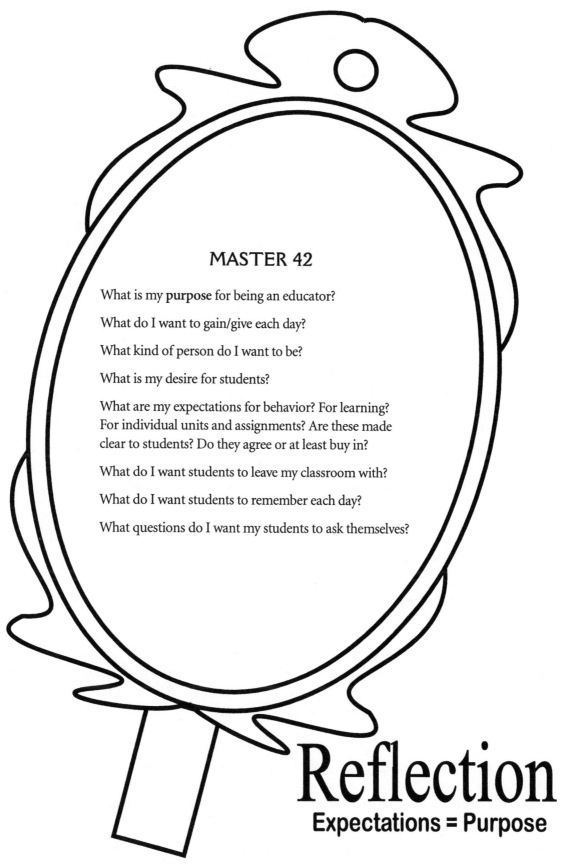

MASTER 42

What is my **purpose** for being an educator?

What do I want to gain/give each day?

What kind of person do I want to be?

What is my desire for students?

What are my expectations for behavior? For learning? For individual units and assignments? Are these made clear to students? Do they agree or at least buy in?

What do I want students to leave my classroom with?

What do I want students to remember each day?

What questions do I want my students to ask themselves?

Reflection
Expectations = Purpose

Procedure = Potential

How can we expect students to know what to do if we don't involve them, show them, teach them? Few of us showed up for the first day of work without any direction, instruction, or preparation. By cooperatively designing procedures for classroom behaviors, you are cocreating the mental movie for students to rehearse/use, a vision of what to do (the **potential**), rather than assuming they already/should know and punishing them when they don't, as is the case with many rules. The best practices to minimize behavior problems are sound classroom procedures that make sense to students, are understood by students, and enable students to be decision makers, assume responsibility, and learn effectively. In fact, positive procedures, the **potentials** to behave appropriately, that are created with and taught to students replace the need for most rules. Student input can be as little or as much as you like. Whether or not students agree, "The fact that they have had the opportunity to express their opinions makes it more likely that they will be able to accept" (Gootman, 1997, p. 39). A useful line building on *past, present,* and *people potentials* is,

> This is the way students have handled _____ (e.g., excuses, handing in papers, bathroom) in the past, and it has worked great. Let me walk you through each step, and then I'll ask for ideas to help make the procedure work best for all of us here now.

For example, makeup work is often a headache for teachers and students alike and the downfall of otherwise decent grades. Following is a procedure for makeup work designed with seventh-grade English students to give them responsibility, me time to take roll, and prevent problems. This procedure worked well, in part, because it was taught as a lesson itself. Of course, you will need to design a **potential** that works for you and your students. There is no such thing as a universal procedure.

Class activities and assignments were written both on the chalkboard and on a clipboard each day. Students would come into class and immediately know what to expect. The first 5 minutes of class were spent writing. A sentence starter, topic, quote, or free write was on the board. The class came in, and the bell meant go (I also taught this procedure complete with practice drills during which a play bell was rung). During this silent time, I would enter the room, take roll, hand out any handouts/returns for the day, and answer any makeup work questions.

Any student who had been absent would consult the clipboard for the day(s) gone and write down exactly what it said—the writing opener, the classtime events, and the assignment. Then if there were any additional input, handouts, or questions, we would have 5 minutes to get them on-line or arrange an additional time to meet. When the time was up, we would all start class together, warmed up and ready.

The instruction was like this: I would walk through the procedure *pretending* I had been absent. Next, I would select a student to narrate and a student to act out the procedure; we would do this several times (10 minutes). The next day, I would have the students *pretend* the person to the right was new and needed the makeup procedure explained to her or him. Then, I would let someone *pretend* she or he had been absent and walk us through the procedure (3 minutes).

Makeup work was never a problem. The students had the responsibility of consulting the clipboard and did so on their own. They were not forced to chase me down and ask that question that all teachers hate: "Did we do anything yesterday?" A few minutes and some fun play-acting ensured that every student had the **potential** to have success with the procedure—and did!

Procedures create an expectancy that predicts success. Rules with detailed consequences create an expectancy for *when* they are broken. I have seen some makeup rules that tell how many points will be lost if the work is not made up in 2 days, almost assuming that it won't be, overlooking any instruction on how to do it at all. The word *rule* is not what makes the difference; the negative expectation is. Solutioning uses *purpose* and *potentials* or *expectations* and *procedures,* but you must use words that work for you and your students. Some students may respond to the word *rule,* with its connotation of power/authority.

Begin developing your students' **potentials** while preventing discipline problems with clear, taught procedures. An excellent solutioning tool to use is the Fab Five criteria: *personal, positive, process, precise,* and *present.* In fact, these can be used conjunctively with students as procedures are required, developed, and evaluated, thus teaching the criteria as well. Use the reflection questions on MASTER 43 "Reflection: Procedures = Potential" alone or with students to begin developing classroom **potentials.** Follow up with MASTER 44 "Language Lesson: Classroom Potentials" using the Fab Five criteria. The Golden Rule—Do unto others as you would have others do unto you—may be the only rule you ever need again.

MASTER 43

What procedures do I currently have that work?

Do I teach them to students?

Are they followed?

What makes them work?

What could I do/teach to make them better?

What procedures could I/we develop to cover areas where problems sometimes arise?

What would my students say about our classroom procedures?

Could I replace any of my rules with a taught procedure?

Could I develop a lesson plan for some procedures I am assuming students know but don't seem to be following?

Reflection
Procedures = Potential

Classroom Potentials

MASTER 44

1. PERSONAL Relevant, applicable, and necessary for/to students	*you*	What will this procedure do for *you?* How will this help *you* learn? What ideas do *you* have for helping our classroom run smoothly?
2. POSITIVE What students will be doing, as opposed to what they will not.	*instead*	What will you be doing *instead* of yelling? What will you be doing for . . . ? How will you leave the room, sharpen pencils, and so on?
3. PROCESS Actions, behaviors	*how, -ing*	What does talk*ing* quietly look like? *How* will you be turn*ing* in your work?
4. PRECISE Clearly specified behaviors	*exactly*	What, *exactly,* will you do next? What does that look like? What does cooperation, respect, and so on look like?
5. PRESENT In the here and now, age/culturally appropriate		When you come to class tomorrow and are using this **potential,** what will you be doing, saying, thinking?

LANGUAGE LESSON

Communication is vital, not only so that the **purpose** is shared and the **potentials** work, but also in building positive interactions with students. Solutioning is also preventive in nature because of the relationship it naturally builds with students. By involving students as partners in so many ways, you are building a climate of respect and trust.

> In the classroom students who feel accepted by their teachers are more likely to do what the teacher asks of them (e.g., assignments) and less likely to do things that make teachers' lives difficult (e.g., disrupt). . . . just take the time to "talk with" and "listen to" students both individually and collectively. (Morganett, 1991, p. 261)

The idea of "talking with" and "listening to" students can be about any area of classroom/school life—for example, curriculum, learning, solving problems, strengths, abilities, needs, content, skills—and is inherent in the solutioning process (see MASTER 45 "Practice Makes Perfect: Discipline? Classroom Management? Solutioning?" and MASTER 46 "Reflection: Solutioning Your Classroom"). Effective interactions do not have to be personal or time-consuming. Going further, Morganett (1991) states that even more important than talking and listening is "the way we talk with and listen to students" (p. 261), which is where solutioning really pays off. The presuppositions of respect, faith, and ability and the assumptions of solutions and success are expressed through the language. Being there with students instead of above them, having dialogues instead of monologues, and interacting as partners make all the difference. Why waste time talking and listening if these do not enhance the learner, the learning environment, and the relationship while decreasing concerns?

By giving input and choice through the language of solutioning, you will not be having to do *to* students, whether that be rewards, punishments, or control. Not having to maintain a position of power, put check marks on the board, stay in during lunch, bribe, and so on saves time, time that can be spent designing creative lessons. Observing students making good choices, working toward solutions, and growing into good learners and quality characters is inspiring; watching for rule breakers is tiring. "Children learn to make good choices by having the chance to choose, not by following directions" (Kohn, 1995, p. 34).

Practice Makes Perfect

DISCIPLINE? CLASSROOM MANAGEMENT? SOLUTIONING?

MASTER 45

Instructions: Look at the following example scenarios and think about how you would normally react and then about how solutioning may fit. How are the two similar, different? Which gives the message, thinking, choice, and responsibility you are striving for in students? Are you controlling, encouraging, doing to? Or interacting with students? What to do?

1. Mark often forgets his books, homework, lunch—you name it. On the morning of a field trip, he forgets to return a signed permission slip. What do you do?

What I would do:

What solutioning could do:

2. George just hit Nadia. What do you do?

What I would do:

What solutioning could do:

3. Marie was cheating on her spelling exam. What do you do?

What I would do:

What solutioning could do:

(continued)

Practice Makes Perfect

DISCIPLINE? CLASSROOM MANAGEMENT? SOLUTIONING?

MASTER 45 Continued

Helpful Hints

1. Use questions to give the student responsibility.
2. Lead the student in reflecting on her or his own behavior.
3. Use solutioning language to form a **purpose for change.**
4. Explore **potentials** to help the student achieve the **purpose.**
5. Make a doable **plan.**

For example:

1.

"Well, Mark, it looks as if forgetting has caused you to miss the field trip. Are there times when you win over forgetting? How do you do that? Great, you have the ability to remember. *When* you do more of that from now on, you'll be going on all of the field trips."

2.

Teacher:	Let's talk about this. Could each of you tell me what's going on?
George:	She took my ball.
Nadia:	I had it first.
Teacher:	Are there times in the past or even now when you share things? (Both nod) How do you do that?
George:	I ask to play with someone or ask to take turns.
Nadia:	Laurie and I just trade off or something.
Teacher:	So, what might be a good **plan** here?
George:	I could tell her that instead of just grabbing it that if she asked we could throw it back and forth.
Nadia:	I guess I could ask to play when I see him with it.
Teacher:	Great ideas. That sounds like a **plan.** Try it for a day and let me know tomorrow how it works.

Practice Makes Perfect

DISCIPLINE? CLASSROOM MANAGEMENT? SOLUTIONING?

MASTER 45 Continued

3.

Teacher: Marie, could we talk?

Marie: Yeah.

Teacher: What might I say is a reason for us to talk?

Marie: You saw me looking on Tate's paper.

Teacher: When don't you look on someone else's paper?

Marie: When I study and know the answers myself.

Teacher: How do you do that—study and do it yourself?

Marie: I take it home the night before, but last night I didn't.

Teacher: So, when you take it home and study, you do the test on your own and know the answers. That sounds like it really works for you.

Marie: Yeah. I wish I would have done that last night.

Teacher: So, from now on when you study and know the answers yourself, you won't be getting zeros for looking on someone else's paper. That sounds like a **plan.** Let's talk again next week, and you can tell me all the ways you study and know the answers for yourself and resist looking on anyone's paper.
OK?

Marie: OK.

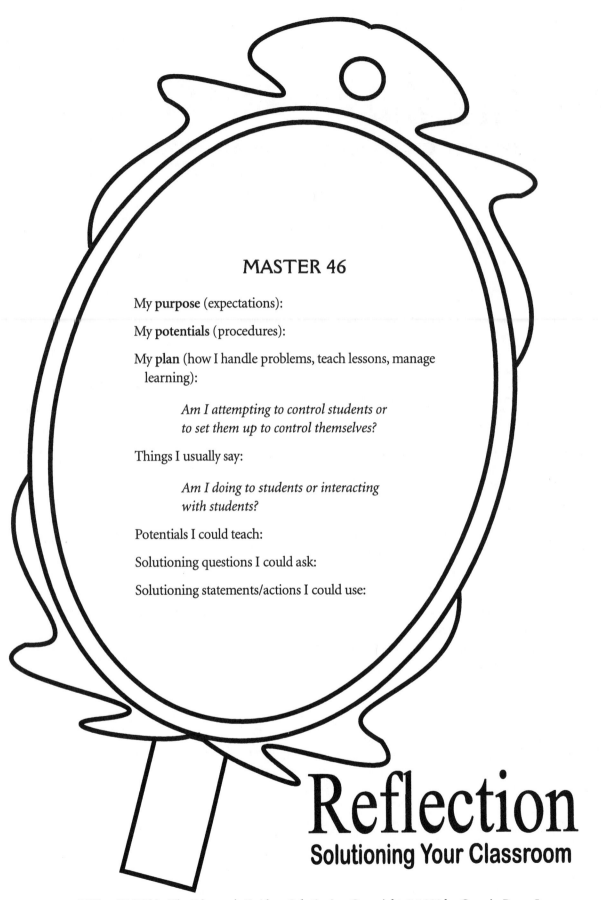

MASTER 46

My **purpose** (expectations):

My **potentials** (procedures):

My **plan** (how I handle problems, teach lessons, manage learning):

Am I attempting to control students or to set them up to control themselves?

Things I usually say:

Am I doing to students or interacting with students?

Potentials I could teach:

Solutioning questions I could ask:

Solutioning statements/actions I could use:

Reflection
Solutioning Your Classroom

Using choice puts students in charge of their learning, builds awareness of how they best learn, and encourages responsibility.

Go Infinity and Beyond

Lesson Planning, Assignments, and Assessment

As the solutioning focus becomes a way of life in your classroom, it will easily blend into your lessons, assignments, and assessments. Looking at each step of the solutioning process as applied to lessons illustrates its research-based applicability. Having a **purpose** for each lesson is perhaps obvious to educators, yet often is unclear for students. The solutioning idea of a *joint purpose* can be used to bring students on board, so to speak. Think about your own education. How motivated were you to learn something in which you saw no value or relevance, no connection? Of course, we are not salespeople and should not have to sell our students on curriculum. A few solutioning questions, however, can lead students in discovering their own reasons for learning. "Students are more likely to approach and engage in learning in a manner consistent with a mastery goal when they perceive meaningful reasons for engaging in a activity . . . and when task presentations emphasize personal relevance and meaningfulness of the content" (Ames, 1992, p. 263).

Having a **purpose**, a reason, an objective developed with or, at the very least, discussed with students not only illustrates that you value them as partners in learning but also sets up a positive expectation and focuses their minds. Objectives help activate a mental set that focuses students' attention and directs selective perception of specific lesson content (Klein & Pridemore, 1994). Use the Fab Five criteria (see MASTER 47 "Reflection: Fab Five Objectives") to create objectives that are doable, observable, and achievable.

Thinking

Journal entry of Cathy Crane, principal (Used with permission from Cathy Crane)

This was during a conference with one of my teachers after a successful lesson. I asked her what she had done differently when preparing this lesson. She shared that she had really spent time focusing on her objective: What did she want the children to be able to do when they were doing the activity? I asked her how she had done this. She had to think for a few seconds. It was a little difficult for her to put into words. We then talked about the importance of *thinking of what exactly she wanted children to be able to do was the best way to begin to focus on the objective.* We talked about how she would think about planning her lesson for the next week, how to keep these successes going (**progress** questions).

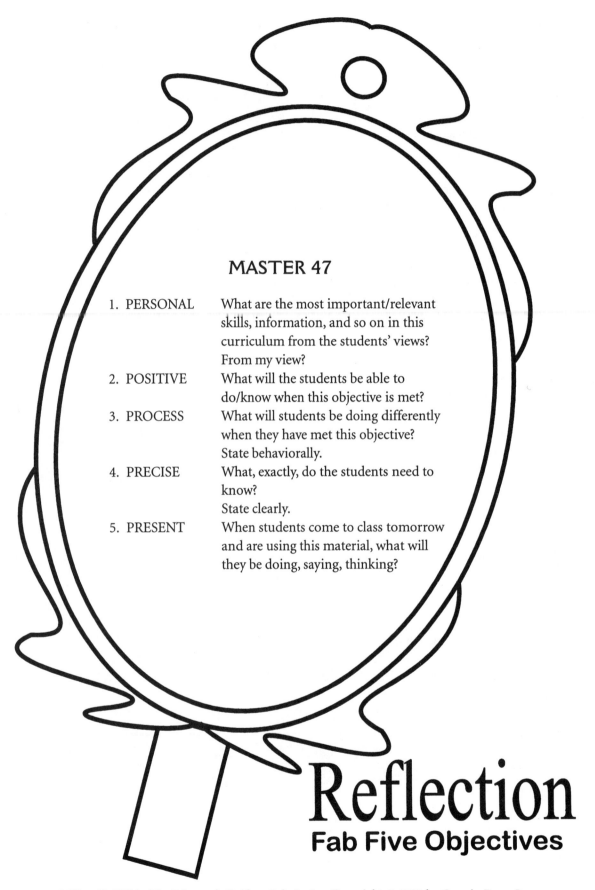

MASTER 47

1. PERSONAL   What are the most important/relevant skills, information, and so on in this curriculum from the students' views? From my view?

2. POSITIVE   What will the students be able to do/know when this objective is met?

3. PROCESS   What will students be doing differently when they have met this objective? State behaviorally.

4. PRECISE   What, exactly, do the students need to know? State clearly.

5. PRESENT   When students come to class tomorrow and are using this material, what will they be doing, saying, thinking?

Reflection
Fab Five Objectives

Approaching your content with variety and diversity, as in the exploration of **potentials,** meets many requirements of effective instruction. Use *past potential* to tie learning into existing information; "relate potentially meaningful information to be learned to existing structures that exist within a learner's memory" (Klein & Pridemore, 1994, p. 42). Use *present potential* to build on existing projects, skills, and abilities. Incorporate *pretend* and *people* to make learning more fun, varied, and applicable. In preparing your presentation, ask yourself some **potential** questions and make the learning diverse enough to connect for all students.

Using choice, as in the **plans** of solutioning, puts students in charge of their learning, builds awareness of how they best learn, and encourages responsibility. "Malone and Lepper (1987; see also Lepper & Hodell, 1989) described challenge, interest, and perceived control as factors that should be embedded in the structure and design of learning tasks" (Ames, 1992, p. 264). The **plans** of solutioning applied to learning tasks empower students to individualize (for themselves), something we know is necessary but find very time-consuming (see MASTER 48 "Solutioning Lesson Design"). Also, to decrease the behavior problems that often stem from inappropriate tasks, put choice in the **plan** for practicing/learning material. "Many behavioral problems occur because students are either bored with an activity that is too easy or frustrated because it is too difficult" (Smith & Riveria, 1995, p. 3).

Take choice one step farther with staggered deadlines. One situation that is annoying for all educators is late assignments and how to handle them. Some teachers are "never take a late paper" types, some are the "unclear or wishy-washy" types that have to listen to lots of excuses, and then there are the proactive, solutioning-focused types. Not appropriate for all assignments but very helpful with larger ones, staggered deadlines give choice. For example, suppose the actual due date is Wednesday. Give 20 points extra credit for those that come in on Monday, 10 points for Tuesday, make Wednesday break-even day, deduct 10 for Thursday, and deduct 20 for Friday. This approach allows the students to make choices. Some may burn the midnight oil for the 20 extra, and some may choose to lose 10 and do their best quality work. The teacher is saved any decision making, excuses, or hassles and gets more time for grading.

Setting up lessons based on the questions of solutioning encourages higher-order thinking, decision making, and student control. The real-life skills gleaned from these processes far outvalue the content or material in most cases. Curriculum mastery, however, is also enhanced with these higher-order processes, and students are better able to apply what they have learned. Notice the **plan** choices in MASTER 48 "Solutioning Lesson Design."

In teaching, it is the method and not the content that is the message . . . the drawing out, not the pumping in. (Ashley Montagu in Peter, 1977, p. 465)

Monitoring **progress** and evaluating and assessing students is the part of the process that makes solutioning circular, ongoing, and full of momentum. The solutioning focus will empower you to approach assessment with a new spark. Emphasizing and building on student competencies and skills are so much more motivating for choosing objectives and planning lessons than trying to fill needs and overcome deficits. End results are the same: student mastery of curriculum.

Use **progress** questions to help students balance formal assessments with the solutioning focus. The questioning, responsibility, and self-esteem-earning stance of the **progress** language blend perfectly with student self-evaluations, which "transform the experience of schooling into meaningful learning" (Eaton & Pougiales, 1993, p. 48). This follows through with the responsible community of learners that has been created. For example, after students have talked about what kind of classroom they want, chosen how they will best practice/learn a lesson, and so on, they must then answer questions like "What did I gain or learn?" "How did I grow?" "What worked?" "What of this can I use to learn more, make my life better, reach a goal?" The personalization of one's own work and reflection about that work help make learning visible and relevant to students and teachers alike (Eaton & Pougiales, 1993). Solutioning has been encouraging responsibility every step of the way. Why take it back when it comes to evaluation of learning? Instead, let students in on what assessment is all about and use it as a learning tool. "Sharing the responsibility for evaluation with students gives them a degree of responsibility for their own education and encourages them to learn something about the nature of evaluation itself" (Eaton & Pougiales, 1993, p. 58).

If students are to earn self-esteem, we must give them a chance to prove their ability to learn to themselves, rather than have them always rely on us as the authorities. By incorporating **progress** questions into every lesson, or at least at the ends of units, we are leaving students with much more than a letter grade. We are helping them personally consider what it is they have gained from their efforts and experience. In essence, we are teaching them control over their learning and encouraging true responsibility in every facet of classroom life and learning. If we are to practice what we preach, we must do so fully by being solutioning focused in all areas.

> "When grades are not the only motivator for participation students often find intrinsic reasons for tackling the material and concepts presented in the course. Additionally, they often begin to recognize their responsibility for experiences in the learning situation" (Eaton & Pougiales, 1993, p. 58).

Having a system where students compete against each other for grades just doesn't fit with solutioning. Instead, each student should be acknowledged for abilities and encouraged to use those to maximize her or his own performance. As Morganett (1996) states, "All students can be successful if their grades are at least partially based on their current knowledge and skills" (p. 149). How can you build on success if you are showing deficits, making grades public, and comparing students? Be respectful of your students at all times. Nothing is more problem focused (and detrimental to learning) than having students grade each others' papers and find each others' mistakes, just to save the teacher time. These teachers most likely are the ones doing the most complaining and blaming in the teacher's lounge.

Using some solutioning questions/ideas within lessons, whether or not you alter any other area, will show respect to students, encourage them take charge of their growth, and facilitate future experiences. For example, simply discussing how learning might continue after the class ends and encouraging students to take their learning **potentials,** competencies, and abilities and do more of what works give the lesson a solutioning focus. MASTER 48 "Solutioning Lesson Design" is a summary of the solutioning-focused lesson; MASTER 49 "Practice Makes Perfect: Solutioning Lesson Design" will give you a chance to try out some of your ideas. Blend in and adapt what you are already using that works. A few questions here and there, and you will be instating solutioning, sure to enhance any lesson.

MASTER 48

Solutioning Lesson Design

PURPOSE—objective. Establish the need for the lesson: the rationale, problem, goal, and so on behind the lesson. Make the lesson applicable by establishing a joint **purpose;** you may need to consider the consequences; uses, careers, tie-ins to other lessons; and so on. This will get the students' minds on the topic, set the mood for learning, and establish ownership.

POTENTIAL—information. Employ instruction, teaching, and modeling, the curriculum portion of the lesson.

> *PAST. Connect the information with something the students already know or have learned or done in the past. This is a perfect area for reviewing and bridging.*

> *PRESENT. Tie the information to something the students are currently learning or doing, other disciplines, real life. Use interdisciplinary units. This is a good area for assimilation of information.*

> *PRETEND. Use visualization, imagery, and imagination by having students see themselves knowing the information and the differences that makes. The information can be tied to the future and made relevant by pretending a future of knowing/using it. This is a good area for repetition of information.*

> *PEOPLE. Relate the information to people by showing how people create, use, or interact with it. Bring the information into the students' reality. Maybe look at how others have learned the information or who can be consulted for additional information/support.*

PLAN—practice. Give the student some choice in the **plan** (practice), knowing how she or he will best be able to master the material.

> *POSITIVE. Notice what information you like, what information will help you, what information you already know, and how it ties into your life now or in the future. This can be done in the form of writing, discussion, and so on.*

> *PRACTICE. Create visualizations (mental and/or concrete, e.g., written, drawn, sung) of themselves doing, knowing, or using the information—for example, planning the experiment, getting the materials for sewing, writing an outline of the visualized piece, acting out being a nurse or a teacher.*

> *PERFORM. Allow demonstrations, presentations, arts, crafts, labs, assignments, projects, and hands-on activities with the information, and illustrations of knowing the information such as tests and portfolios.*

PROGRESS. Use continually the information as it relates to future lessons, future plans, and so on. Celebrate the knowing of the information by looking at results and considering what was learned and how so that it can be applied to future learning. Evaluate what was learned and what worked in the lesson. Student self-evaluations fit perfectly here.

Practice Makes Perfect

SOLUTIONING LESSON DESIGN

MASTER 49

PURPOSE. What is the **purpose** of teaching this lesson? What should students be able to do as a result? How will they benefit? What **purpose** do they have for learning this?

_____

_____

_____

POTENTIALS

PAST. What do the students already know, or what abilities do they have that can be used, tied to, built upon for this lesson?

_____

_____

_____

PRESENT. How does this information fit with other areas of learning, life, and so on? How can I best relate this information in the students' present realities?

_____

_____

_____

PRETEND. Could the students use visualization to see themselves using this information, whether it is on a test or in their future? How can I use imagery and imagination in presenting this information?

_____

_____

_____

(continued)

Practice Makes Perfect
SOLUTIONING LESSON DESIGN

MASTER 49 Continued

PEOPLE. How can this information be socialized for the students? How do people use it, interact with it, create it? How have others learned or applied this information that I can share? Who can be used as a resource or support of this lesson?

_____

_____

_____

PLAN. Will the students choose? Will all three types be used in some way?

POSITIVE. Could I ask students what they already know, how this fits, what they like, what is useful?

PRACTICE. What visualizations (mental or physical) of the material could be used for practice?

PERFORM. What tasks could the students use to best learn, apply the material?

_____

_____

_____

PROGRESS. How will this best be evaluated? What questions could students ask themselves? What was learned? How can it be used again, more?

_____

_____

_____

It should be obvious by now that every aspect of solutioning encourages thinking and decision making. Whether you use solutioning solely as your problem-solving process or fully adapt the solutioning focus into all aspects of life and learning, one result will be students who can think. According to Sparks (1993), "To promote good decision-making skills, the teacher must develop a sense of trust, while allowing students opportunities to make personal decisions" (p. 75). In accordance with this thought, the focus of solutioning provides the trust and the language and the opportunity. Within this environment, critical thinking is bound to happen—from problem solving, to decision making regarding learning, to self-reflection. All of this and no new curriculum.

Critical Thinking, Decision Making, and Lifelong Learning

Learning succeeds to the degree that it gradually assists the learner to take control of his or her own learning process. (Eaton & Pougiales, 1993, p. 55)

The solutioning focus is illustrated through the environment you present. Focusing on the positive begins with comfort, ease, and politeness. When the basic needs are met, solutions are more easily created and enacted. Beyond the basic needs, visual aids, direct instruction, and modeling are powerful tools for spreading the solutioning focus.

A Setting for Solutioning

Classroom walls can serve as billboards for solutioning. Choose your favorite questions and put them up for student reflection and/or as a personal reminder. Quote the focus; have bulletin boards of positive events, accomplishments, problem exceptions, and usable **potentials**. Encourage students to find the good news among the bad, the growth despite the struggles. Display these positives and begin solutioning habits for all. Some poster ideas are provided in MASTERS 50, 51, and 52. Please use them and send me yours.

Solutioning
Willyn Webb, MA, LPC, NCC
117 Meeker St., #7
Delta, CO 81416

An obvious route to helping create solutioning-focused environments and learners is to teach students the 3-P process and the language of solutioning. With older learners, this book may serve your needs. Younger students are also very capable of learning solutioning, first as their problem-solving method and second as their focus tool. Various level of curricula for teaching solutioning to students will be available soon.

"In both conscious and unconscious ways, students see each and every teacher behavior as a **potential** behavior that they may adopt for themselves" (Tierno, 1998, p. 59). Remember the comparison charts. Which side do you want or feel obligated to model? Which side do you prefer that students be on? If we yell at students, they will yell at us. If we hand papers back later than we said we would, students will turn in late assignments. If we focus on deficits, students will know what they can't do and what we can't do. Is this what you want to have happening in your classroom setting? Now think of the solutioning sides of the charts. If students reflected back to you these types of behaviors, can you visualize what a wonderful setting would result? Very simply, "It is the teacher's own behaviors that appear to be the singularly most significant variable in determining the extent to which a classroom environment positively contributes to the social growth [and learning behaviors] of students" (Tierno, 1998, p. 58).

Chapter 6 Focused

The difference that can be made in classroom management, discipline, and lessons with just a few questions is incredible.

Why stop now? As you can see, the difference that can be made in classroom management, discipline, and lessons with just a few questions is powerful. Blend in and adapt what you are already doing. Make the language fit you and your students. Start with one question and go from there. You will notice a difference that is sure to supercharge the development of your classroom's and/or school's solutioning focus.

MASTER 50

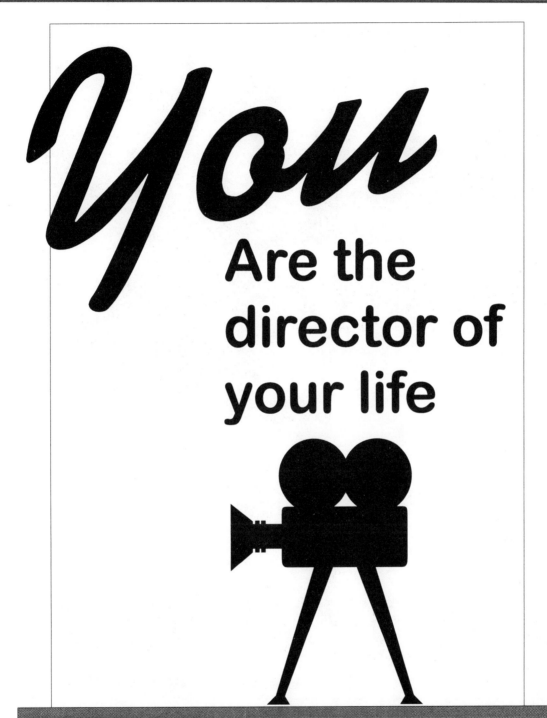

MASTER 51

MASTER 52

7

The Adventure Continues

Solutioning Conflict, Parents, and Meetings

By now, it is obvious that solutioning is an empowered focus; a modus operandi that positively affects all aspects of life—even those sometimes challenging aspects of conflict, parents, and meetings. Once solutioning is blended into your personal script, you will find yourself using it in most interactions; thus, the adventure continues.

Solutioning will speed the conflict resolution process, motivate the participants, and prevent many conflicts from ever surfacing.

Peace at Last: Solutioning Conflict

From the "She took my pencil" of elementary school to the "He called me a blank" of middle school to the "I'm going to kick your blankety-blank" of high school, at times every teacher finds the learning environment interrupted by conflict. Karen Birgam, a social studies teacher at Northeast High School in Kansas City, Missouri, states, "Ninety percent of the conflicts at Northeast are of the 'he said, she said' variety, which students are well-equipped to handle. However, gone unchecked, those are also the kind that can escalate into full-blown fights" (cited in Hancock, 1994, p. 9).

Conflict management is a must as a rising tide of violence is plaguing our schools. Many programs are available that offer both conflict resolution and conflict mediation. Results are encouraging: "The frequency of student-student conflicts teachers had to manage dropped 80 percent after the training and the number of conflicts referred to the principal was reduced by 95 percent" (Johnson & Johnson, 1996, p. 17). Solutioning can enhance a program already in place or be expanded into a conflict resolution/mediation program itself. The language makes the difference, as Terry Killin, principal; and Rhonda Williams, counselor; at Thunder Ridge Middle School in Aurora,

Colorado, share: "School climate is affected dramatically when students learn to resolve conflicts through communication rather than through violence" (Killin & Williams, 1995, p. 46).

Conflict resolution is a tool needed by all students, teachers, and schools (and spouses, and employees, and parents, and so on). As Johnson and Johnson (1996) point out,

> Conflicts will not go away. Students are clearly fascinated by and drawn to conflicts—they like to start them, watch them, hear about them, and discuss them. In order to make schools orderly and peaceful places in which high-quality education can take place, conflicts must be managed constructively without physical or verbal violence. (p. 11)

We want students to enter our classrooms, feeling at ease rather than afraid, relaxed rather than nervous, and sure rather than unsure of what will happen during their day. If students know what to expect and what to do when conflict occurs, they not only will put their minds on learning but may even learn from conflict as well. Relationships and self-esteem improve. As we consider the general objectives for school-based conflict resolution programs, you will see how solutioning has it covered, so to speak:

1. Promoting a more receptive and responsive view of conflict as a positive force that can accompany personal growth or institutional change

2. Helping young people, school personnel, and community members deepen their understanding of themselves and others through improved communication, thereby improving school climate and preparing students to live in a multicultural world

3. Increasing appreciation for the ability of conflict resolution training to enhance academic and lifetime skills considered basic to all learning, such as listening, critical and creative thinking, and problem solving

4. Encouraging a higher level of citizenship activity by sharpening students' knowledge of nonadversarial conflict resolution, its relationship to the U.S. legal system, and the role it can play in promoting world peace

5. Recognizing the unique competence of young people to participate in the resolution of their own disputes while allowing teachers and administrators to concentrate more on teaching and less on discipline

6. Offering a more appropriate and effective school-based dispute resolution method than expulsion, suspension, detention, or court intervention and thus reducing violence, vandalism, and chronic school absences (Davis, 1986)

Chart 7.1 Conflict Resolution

Problem-Focused, Traditional	*Solutioning-Focused*
"This is what happened . . ." (preliminary to stating the problem)	Share views—externalize the problem
"This is why I think it happened . . ." (preliminary to stating the problem)	
"The problem is . . ." (state the problem)	
"These are ways I can help it from not happening again." (brainstorm)	Explore **potentials:**
	"When have things been better in the past? What were you doing, saying, thinking differently?"
	"When are things OK now? What is different?"
	"Pretend this is solved. What are you doing differently?"
	"How would others solve this?"
"This is what I choose to do so that it won't happen again." (select a solution)	"On the basis of what you've just shared that works, what could you do more of, try, or borrow?" "Choose a plan that meets the Fab Five criteria."

Conflict resolution using traditional problem-solving steps is effective. Solutioning, however, will speed the process, motivate the participants, and prevent many conflicts from ever surfacing. Traditional problem-solving methods of resolving conflict spend a great deal of time talking about the problem, whereas solutioning leads quickly and directly to solutions. The focus shifts like a playground seesaw. Look at the comparison in Chart 7.1. The problem-focused side is based on traditional problem solving-steps to resolve conflict in Gootman (1997) and P.A.C.E., a student problem-solving procedure in Campbell (1995).

In solutioning negotiation/mediation, participants team up against a problem and coconstruct solutions. The tools from Chapter 2 are used to distinguish the problem as a separate entity. By externalizing the problem, the battle is not between people, but against a problem. This approach often douses the fires of competition between disputants and propels them toward the next step.

Whereas many programs require "generating at least three optional agreements that would maximize the benefits for both parties," they give little direction on how to "generate," which is often where many students get stuck and much time is wasted (Johnson & Johnson, 1996, p. 15). It is difficult to pull ideas out of thin air, out of young, inexperienced minds, out of students who have lived in violence. When two parties are in conflict, often the idea of the other (no matter what it is) is most repulsive just because of who came up with it. The **potentials** questions give students ways to "generate" solution ideas together.

Questioning *past* and *present* exceptions, creating *pretend* visions, and borrowing ideas from other *people* empower students to explore, which leads to solutions. In answering the questions, solutions usually become obvious, and the need to evaluate alternatives (often leading to feelings of rejection) is eliminated. The solution is actually coconstructed because the exploration is guided and structured. Rather than trying to generate a solution, students get to share information that builds solutions, a less demanding and more productive process.

But, She Said . . .

Sheryl was an eighth-grader with some solutioning training. Fatima and Bambi had been taught "I" messages and restating. They wanted to solve the problem, so that was helpful. Tougher cases with more anger require additional questions. With Sheryl using the worksheet [MASTER 54 "Solutioning Mediation"] to mediate the conflict, I was able to get a lot of work done, and the girls were very proud of the solution they jointly discovered.

Sheryl brought Fatima and Bambi into the counselor's office, crying and upset. Sheryl said they were in a big fight and almost hit each other during lunch. Fatima broke in, "She called me a sl_t."

Bambi interrupted, "Everybody told me you wanted to kick my a__."

This time, I interjected, "Do you want to work this out?" and I got nods from all three. I got out the mediation sheet, handed it to Sheryl, and said I would be working on the computer if they should need me. They were sitting right outside my door, where I could hear every word.

Sheryl: Each of you needs to share your side of the story by using "I" messages. Listen to each other and restate.

Fatima: I feel mad because she called me a sl_t and I'm not. I don't even have a boyfriend.

Sheryl: OK, Bambi, you restate how Fatima is feeling.

Bambi: She's mad because of what I called her. Well, I feel pissed off when everybody keeps coming up to me and saying she's going to kick my a__. I thought we were friends.

Sheryl: Fatima, how is Bambi feeling?

Fatima: She's mad 'cause of what people have been telling her, but I never said that.

Sheryl: So, the problem is what has been said. Do you want to be friends? (Both nod) OK, when are things better?

Bambi: When everyone else isn't telling me stuff.

Fatima: Yeah, when I hear what she has said, I don't know who to believe.

Sheryl: So, when you talk to each other instead of listening to others, this doesn't happen. (Both nod) How have you done that—listened only to each other?

Bambi: Last year, this almost happened, but the teacher had me ask Fatima if she had said it before I believed it and got mad.

Sheryl: So, when you ask each other first, it keeps you from getting mad?

Fatima: Yeah.

Sheryl: Let's meet in 1 week and talk about it. Bambi, you go directly to Fatima and ask about what you've heard before getting mad. And Fatima, you go directly to Bambi and ask about what you've heard before getting mad. OK?

MASTER 53 "Solutioning Negotiation" and MASTER 54 "Solutioning Mediation" are forms that can be used for solutioning negotiation or for solutioning mediation. You may choose to adapt the language to fit the developmental level of your students and/or your conflict resolution or peer mediation program(s) already in place.

It's not uncommon to see students at Bode using mediation skills in the hallways and on the school grounds. You know with feedback like that, you've taught a life skill. (Suzanne Lehr, middle school teacher, in Hancock, 1994, p. 10)

MASTER 53

Solutioning Negotiation

PURPOSE

1. Students share their view/story/**purpose.** This does not have to be extensive or time-consuming, just enough to hear/understand each others' views. Some ground rules may be helpful:

     Use "I" messages.
     Listen, then restate.
     Agree to stay until a **plan** is created.

   Student 1's story:

   _____

   _____

   _____

   Student 2's story:

   _____

   _____

   _____

2. Externalize the concern as separate from either one of the persons; agree on a name for it.

   _____

   _____

   _____

3. Consider the results/consequences of keeping (externalized problem) and of finding a solution. If we continue with (externalized problem), this might happen:

   Student 1:

   _____

   _____

   _____

(continued)

MASTER 53 Continued

Student 2:

_____

_____

_____

If we use a solution this might happen:

Student 1:

_____

Student 2:

_____

_____

_____

POTENTIALS

1. When have you not had (the externalized problem), or when has it been better? What did each of you do differently then?

Student 1:

_____

_____

_____

Student 2:

_____

_____

_____

MASTER 53 Continued

2. When is (the externalized problem) not happening now, or when is it better? What does each of you do differently?

   Student 1:

   _____

   _____

   _____

   Student 2:

   _____

   _____

   _____

3. *Pretend* this is solved. What would that look like? What would each of you be doing differently?

   Student 1:

   _____

   _____

   _____

   Student 2:

   _____

   _____

   _____

4. How do others solve (the externalized problem)? Who could help you solve this?

   Student 1:

   _____

   _____

   _____

(continued)

MASTER 53 Continued

Student 2:

_____

_____

_____

PLAN

1. Of all the solution ideas above, which one do you want to use for the next _____ days?

Student 1:

_____

_____

_____

Student 2:

_____

_____

_____

The agreed-on **plan** is . . .

_____

_____

In case of a roadblock, we will . . .

_____

_____

We will discuss our success on (date) _____

_____   _____
Student 1 signature   Date

_____   _____
Student 2 signature   Date

MASTER 54

Solutioning Mediation

Following the Journey Through Solutioning Map throughout this process is advised so that students see where the questioning is leading and the structure is visual, obvious, and consistent

Use "I" messages.
Listen to each other, and then restate.

1. PURPOSE

Each student needs an opportunity to share. This does not need to be extensive. The rules of communication must be stressed and enforced. In the restatement, you will want to *normalize, temporize,* or *labelize.*

Student 1: Story, Problem, **Purpose**
Mediator restatement (reflect feeling)

_____

_____

Student 2: Story, Problem, **Purpose**
Mediator restatement (reflect feeling)

_____

_____

Externalize the problem. During the storytelling, the problem will become clear. It is the mediator's job to name the problem (either through questioning participants or individually). The problem must be separate from either of the people. Objectify and personify.

Externalized problem:

_____

To establish the **purpose,** ask whether the participants want to solve the problem.* Using questions about consequences may be helpful in motivating them toward solutions. What will be the results of keeping/solving the problem?

Joint **purpose:**

_____

> *The participants may say they do not want to solve the problem. If that is the case, details of the behaviors of not being friends, not getting along, not agreeing, and so on without continued conflict, threats, or violence are discussed as the solution.*

MASTER 54 Continued

2. POTENTIALS

Ask the following questions and record any **potential** solutions that are shared. Get behavioral details of likely **potentials.** Reword questions as needed, remember to ask and re-ask, and give wait time.

When are things better? What is each of you doing differently then?

For example: When are you friends (e.g., not fighting)? When are you talking nicely, acting trustful, telling the truth, and so on? How do you do that?

Pretend things are better. What is each of you doing differently? How do you want it to be? What does that look like?

For example: What kinds of friends say "Hi," eat lunch together, play football together, call each other or go over?

What ideas for solving this conflict can you borrow from others?

For example: How do your other friends avoid fistfights? What ideas would the teacher have?

Potential answers:

Past exceptions

_____

_____

_____

Present exceptions

_____

_____

_____

Pretend visions

_____

_____

_____

People ideas

_____

_____

_____

MASTER 54 Continued

---

3. PLAN

Summarize the solution(s) gleaned from the **potentials,** being very specific about what is going to happen. See that a time element is jointly chosen. The assumption that the **plan** will happen MUST be in the language.

For example:

Let's meet in _____ days and talk about how you (have Student 1 share **plan**)

_____

_____

_____

and you (have Student 2 share **plan**)

_____

_____

_____

so that things are better.

> *Considering possible roadblocks may be helpful; include a **plan** to use in case one person thinks the other is not completing his or her part of the **plan**. Possibly return to mediation. This breaks patterns and builds in a follow-up system, rather than escalates into violence.*

A SCALING question may be useful:

1	2	3	4	5	6	7	8	9	10

Example questions for the mediator to ask:
Where are you now?
What would you both be doing differently if you moved up just 1 step?
How will you know when things are slightly better?
How are you doing some of that now?

> *All involved may want to sign the written **plan** and make it official. Copies may be made for all involved or the original kept in a neutral place for use when monitoring **progress**, future reference, updates, and so on.*

_____   _____

_____   _____

_____   _____

MASTER 54 Continued

Progress

What worked? How did you do it? How will each of you continue?

Student 1

_____

_____

_____

Student 2

_____

_____

_____

Chart 7.2   Parents

Problem-Focused	Solutioning-Focused
Cause of student problems	Source in solving problems
Adversaries	Allies
Blaming, defending	Exceptions, desires
Parent, teacher, or student seen as the problem	Externalized problem
Directives	Cocreated solutions, **plans**

With a solutioning focus, you will continually be noticing what works, what can be used as a resource, and what is best for your students. Thus, you will be acknowledging the value of parents in aiding students' learning, growing, and behaving. Parents can serve as a tool for finding out when and where students have had success but are often overlooked, labeled, or blamed. Why not use the power of the family to enhance our teaching rather than as an excuse? As Simmons (1991) states, "Parents are the bedrock of the American public schools. They are also one of the school's most neglected and underutilized resources. No one has the vested interest in America's children that parents have" (p. 120). As your focus shifts from problems to solutions (see Chart 7.2), parents will be seen as sources of **potential** solutions, visionaries of positive futures, and teammates.

> **Love Those Parents**

Joint **purposes** will be carried from the student-teacher relationship to the student-teacher-parent relationship. Effective communication, partnerships, and problem prevention always provide the best solutions. Being solutioning focused means never waiting to communicate with parents until a problem appears. Share an exception, an accomplishment, a skill, and/or **progress** with every parent within the first few weeks of school and establish a positive pattern of exceptional communication, the type needed during solutioning, if it ever becomes necessary. This can be done in a form letter on your computer where the exceptional remark is simply changed for each student as the names and addresses are; a quick, two-line handwritten personal note as you observe a positive in class or while grading papers; or a telephone call home. A quick hang-up is key to making the telephone call effective. The positive is shared and the **purpose** fulfilled without a long conversation. Two or three parents could be contacted each evening or messages left on answering machines during the day. MASTER 55 "Language Lesson: Potentials for Parents" provides samples using the guidelines for solution statements (Chapter 5).

The parents were so impressed that I took the time to share a positive that they were more helpful all year. (Delaine Hudson, high school teacher; used with permission from Delaine Hudson)

Potentials for Parents

MASTER 55

Computer Example

Dear (parents'/guardians' names):

I just had to let you know that (student name) _____ (e.g., student accomplishment, skill, ability, **progress**) this week. I am so impressed. You might ask (student name) how he/she does that. I can't help but wonder how you manage to be the type of parent that produces this type of (e.g., person, student, character). You must really be proud.

(teacher's signature)

Telephone Call or Message

This is Mrs. Webb. I noticed your son Matalino really concentrating hard today. Just wanted to let you know how impressed I am. Bye.

Handwritten Examples

Just wanted to share that Ryan completed his task today. Ask him about it. I am impressed.

Mrs. Webb

Cassy stayed in her seat all morning. I'm impressed. How do you think she managed to concentrate so long?

Mrs. Webb

LANGUAGE LESSON

Chart 7.3 Conferences

Problem-Focused	Solutioning-Focused
"The problem is . . ."	"What do you see that is working?"
"This is what needs to be done . . ."	"How do you want things to work?"
Teacher authority/expert	Partnerships
Student absent	Student present, possibly student-led
Blaming, excuses	**Potentials**, exceptions
Past focus, causes	Future focus, solutions

Preparing the contacts is an exercise for educators in observing what works, listening for exceptions, and observing positives. After you have found and acknowledged at least one ability, positive attribute, or skill in each of your students, you will never look at them the same again. Remember, not a single student can have poor academic skills and/or negative behavior 100% of the time. Opening parents' eyes to this fact may begin a change that has a ripple effect. Start **potentials**-based conversations between students and their parents through your positive contact. Solutioning can make a difference before you even know it.

The student-led conference makes students experts over their behaviors and abilities by giving students responsibility.

Solutioning Conferences

The time spend initially in inviting, meeting with, and communicating with parents will save you hours and headaches in the long run as student problems are prevented, quickly solved, and *you* are not the one responsible. Whether or not you choose to take full advantage of the previous suggestions, making parent-teacher conferences the best they can be for all involved means solutioning them. Parent-teacher conferences may be the only face-to-face contact you have with parents, and you must capitalize on the opportunity. Which type of conference do you see as more productive (see Chart 7.3)? More likely to form useful relationships? Which would you like to have?

Forward-focused conferences follow the 3-Ps of solutioning. Add *plural, prepared, private,* and *polite* to make conferences enjoyable, effective, and exceptional in their own right. The solutioning focus is based on the belief that all are worthy and capable. It strives to build empowerment, partnerships, and responsibility. Thus, the most effective conferences are *plural,* involving students. We contradict ourselves by talking about students without them there. Let's not give mixed messages.

Sometimes parents come to conferences without their child even when his or her presence was requested. If this is the case, you must have a conference with the student at a later date, show him or her the notes from the parent conference, and ask for input. The **plan** must be adjusted accordingly if necessary.

Many schools are having great success with student-led conferences (Denby, 1995; Enoch, 1995; Moyers, 1994). The student-led conference fits perfectly with solutioning by making students experts over their behaviors and abilities, by giving students responsibility, and by reinforcing the solutioning process they are learning and using. MASTER 56 "Student Worksheet: Parent Conferences" uses the 3-Ps and will help students prepare to lead their own conferences regardless of their age.

Parent Conferences

MASTER 56

Answer these questions and be ready to share your answers at the conference. Select a few questions/create your own to ask your parent(s)/teacher.

Purpose: What do you want to accomplish with your parent(s), teacher(s)? Communicate/share? Get out of the time together? Talk about?

_____

_____

_____

_____

What is the best way to state this **purpose** to your parent(s)?

_____

_____

_____

_____

Potentials: What do you want to show your parent(s) that you can do? What accomplishments, abilities, successes would you like to share?

Past: What have you done/learned this semester that is important to share?

_____

_____

_____

_____

(continued)

Parent Conferences

MASTER 56 Continued

Present: What are you doing/learning right now that you can tell your parent(s) about or involve them with?

_____

_____

_____

Pretend: How do you want things to be from now on? What do you want to learn more, *practice* more, explore?

_____

_____

_____

People: How might you be assisted in your learning by your parent(s)? By your teacher? By others? Who has helped you already, and how?

_____

_____

_____

Plan: Make a **plan** to achieve your learning vision together.

On the back of this sheet, write down the questions you would like to ask at the conference.

Examples of student work will aid both in externalizing the problem and in providing exceptions, skills, and **potential** solution ideas, so be prepared. Invite parents to share what they find that is working. Begin the conference with a request to discuss what is going right as a means to solve what is not. This approach lets parents in on the focus of solutioning and sets a tone conducive to good communication. In fact, giving parents and students a chance to prepare really starts you all off on an equal footing. MASTER 57 "Let's Be Prepared" is an example you may want to share with students and parents prior to the conference itself.

MASTER 57

Let's Be Prepared

Dear _____ :

Just wanted to remind you that our conference is on _____ (date) at _____ (time). We can meet in Room _____. Please take a few minutes to answer the following questions together with _____ (student's name). Your responses will help us have the best conference possible.

What have you and the student most liked about this school year?

_____

_____

_____

_____

_____

What successes—academic, social, or otherwise—have you all experienced this year?

_____

_____

_____

_____

_____

What of the above can we use to solve any concerns that may come up?

_____

_____

_____

_____

_____

Please return this completed form to me by (date). Thank you! See you soon!

"Privacy is important, so make sure that you have a place where parents can discuss without intrusion" (Simmons, 1991, p. 121). Show respect by providing a setting that is comfortable, quiet, and private and with chairs that fit all sizes. If you want parents to share, give them a solutioning-focused environment in which to do so.

Listen to what parents have to say. Use the "building a strong foundation skills" from Chapter 2 to reflect feeling and meaning. In other words, be polite. Listen for exceptions, positives, and **potential** solutions. When you're sure the parents and the student feel heard, summarize what they have said by pointing out with a solution statement what **potentials** you have heard. When problems are brought up, reflect and follow with a question such as, "So, there are things to work on. Now, let's discuss what tools, skills, abilities, and exceptions we might be able to use. What good things do you see happening?"

Being polite is summed up very well by Simmons (1991):

When a parent is talking, don't interrupt. Seek to understand the parent's feelings, ask questions about what the parent has said and ask them to verify that you have understood them. Never argue with a parent. Respond to a parent's feelings with calmness and understanding. Maintain a position of humility; remember, we only know the child that sits in our classroom and not the one that lives at home. (p. 121)

Of course, when an upset, complaining, or blaming parent comes in and interrupts you during your opening statement with a long discourse on unfairness, on the weaknesses of the child, on why things are not acceptable, and on and on, your natural instincts push you to defend. After you have listened patiently for long enough, the solutioning response is to restate and reflect, rather than defend. This is a crucial statement in setting up a relationship in which you and the parent and, one hopes, the student are working together, rather than against each other.

Harvard Bound

It was conference night, and the parents were free to come in whenever it was convenient for them. This often resulted in long waiting lines outside teachers' rooms, a lack of privacy, and more frustration than desired by anyone. Harold had been waiting patiently in the hall for a while with his daughter Jill. He was leaning against the wall; she was staring at the floor. As soon as it was their turn, Harold came in forcefully (Jill following with eyes to the floor) and interrupted my greeting:

Harold: You sent home a note that said Jill could do so much good work. You said she had impressed you and now you gave her a B on her report card. That's bull___. How's she going to get into Harvard with a B?

My natural reaction would have been to explain that she could do great things and was a very capable child but that two missing assignments from her absences had pulled her grade down and that I was sure it would be an A by semester, which is what is recorded on the permanent records anyway. This would have been defending myself, however, and blaming Jill (who was already trying to hide). I stuck with solutioning, and I'm really glad I did.

Educator: Mr. White, it sounds like you are frustrated that Jill's grade is a B. You see her as capable of an A and would like her to attend Harvard someday. Wow, that is a really admirable goal. (restate and reflect) I agree that Jill has full ability to receive an A. Jill, what grade do you think you can earn? (lead toward joint purpose)

Jill: I want an A.

So I continued.

Educator: So, we all have the same **purpose** here, to talk about how Jill's grade can be an A by semester. What skills, abilities, and habits does Jill have that will get her the A? (joint **purpose, potentials** question)

We went on to discuss all of Jill's wonderful qualities. While exploring *people potential* ideas, Jill shared that doing makeup work when absent was an idea she could borrow. We ended in a few more questions with a **plan** for Jill's father to encourage and help her attend school regularly, for Jill to do her makeup work the next day when absent, and for me to continue letting Jill and her father know of all the wonderful things Jill would be doing to get that A, answer any of her questions, and help with makeup work in any way I could.

Thank goodness we teamed up, especially for Jill. Jill seemed to feel a lot of pressure from Dad, and I am so glad that by defending myself I didn't team up with Dad against Jill, making her feel guilty for not doing makeup work, defending herself, and finding excuses for missing in the first place. She took more responsibility by being given the respect and opportunity for input. She did have an A by semester, by the way.

Because parents often do have some concerns when they come to conferences and it is such valuable time, let's *practice* restating and reflecting, developing a joint **purpose,** and leading into **potentials** on MASTER 58 "Practice Makes Perfect: Parent Conferences." Conferences are the Super Bowl of the blame game. Use solutioning as the best offense—for you, for the parents, and most of all, for the students.

Practice Makes Perfect
PARENT CONFERENCES

MASTER 58

Instructions: Read through the following scenarios from conferences. Avoid your tendencies to defend, make excuses, or blame. Instead, restate and reflect, look for a **purpose** the parent has that you can share, and lead into the exploration of **potential** solutions.

"Caitlin is grounded for the rest of the year. I can't believe she got a C. This has never happened before. You must not be explaining things in a way she can understand, and she's not doing all of her work. She is going to sit at that table every night from now on, and you need to explain things better."

Restate meaning and reflect feeling:

_____

_____

_____

What is a possible joint **purpose?**

_____

_____

_____

What is a possible lead into **potentials?**

_____

_____

_____

"I feel so bad that Billy is getting a D. He's a smart boy, and its all my fault. I've gotten divorced lately, and we are really struggling. We just moved here and don't have any money yet. Billy is really helping out at home, but I know he misses his father, that no-good bum. I have two jobs and am never there to help with the homework. He can get better grades."

(continued)

Practice Makes Perfect

PARENT CONFERENCES

MASTER 58 Continued

Restate meaning and reflect feeling:

_____

_____

_____

What is a possible joint **purpose?**

_____

_____

_____

What is a possible lead into **potentials?**

_____

_____

_____

"I can't believe he's got a C. Aren't you doing your job? My son always tries very hard in class and is a hard worker. There must be something wrong here at school. I never have trouble with him at home. His dad thought he should be held responsible for his grade, but I think it must be you."

Restate meaning and reflect feeling:

_____

_____

_____

What is a possible joint **purpose?**

_____

_____

_____

Practice Makes Perfect

PARENT CONFERENCES

MASTER 58 Continued

What is a possible lead into **potentials?**

_____

_____

_____

"When I was in school, things were different. We didn't do all this cooperative group stuff. We sat in our desks with our mouths shut and did our work. (to his son) Are you causing problems in class? You better not be, or you'll really get it when we get home. What's the matter with ya? You should be passing this class. You must be acting lazy again."

Restate meaning and reflect feeling:

_____

_____

_____

What is a possible joint **purpose?**

_____

_____

_____

What is a possible lead into **potentials?**

_____

_____

_____

Parent Conferences: Before and After

I'll never forget my first parent-teacher conferences. I was so prepared, so nervous, and so inexperienced. Typically, I talk more when nervous. However, I think I was a little apprehensive about allowing the parents to talk, which made it even worse. As you can guess, I had so much to talk about and show that the parents barely got a word in edgewise. I missed out on a great deal of information, insight, and a recruiting opportunity that would have helped me be a better teacher and my students better taught. After using solutioning during conferences, I notice that I do not go home with a dry throat or a headache, but a sense of empowerment, knowing more about how to teach my students, being less responsible, and being part of something bigger than before. What a difference!

The questioning stance, language, and sharing of solutioning automatically sets up a cooperative environment where great ideas will surface and students will benefit. Reassure parents that the problem is not the child, but rather some externalized behavior, situation, or need. During **potentials** (focusing them on things that work), parents get to assume the expert role by sharing their vast past experience with the child. The **plan** flows directly from the **potentials,** so parents are involved in creating it. Simple questions like "How do you want things to be?" and "What exceptions can we build on?" provide a shared **purpose,** an opportunity for everyone to have input in the vision of solutions, and a cocreated **plan.** Educators need only summarize, write it down, and propose a time frame for monitoring **progress,** which should be done no matter what—in writing, by telephone, or with another conference. A form can be used to involve parents in monitoring **progress,** thus continuing the partnership that has begun. An example is found in MASTER 60 "Let's Celebrate Progress."

With good solutioning habits, conferences will not only require very little preparation and effort but also be something you look forward to and enjoy.

> Giving parents a sense of participation and promoting a bond of cooperation between the parent and yourself [and the student] will result in conferences which are less anxious and adversarial and more focused on improving the quality of instruction for the child [at home and school]. (Simmons, 1991, p. 122)

MASTER 59 "Educator Helpsheet: Teacher, Parent, Student Conference," a guide sheet for conferences, will give you confidence during the first few. After that, the language will become automatic and a notepad will serve your needs. Read through it and visualize yourself having this conversation with one or two of your current parents. Can you see yourself using the language and ideas? How does it feel? Make a mental movie of yourself having a wonderful solutioning conference, and you're ready to go.

Remember!

Be Plural: Involve the student whenever you can.

Be Prepared: Have evidence of **potential.**

Be Private: Schedule the conference for a convenient time and place.

Be Polite: Listen to the parent, restate, reflect, and lead.

Use the solutioning 3-P process!

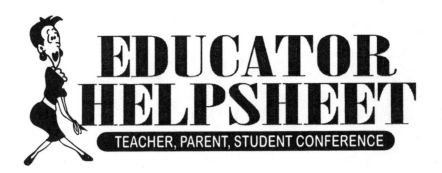

MASTER 59

Begin with solution statements, exceptions, and **potential** solutions. Then they are in place if any problems are brought up. Perhaps have a few of your favorite solutioning questions ready for each area of the process.

"I've asked you here today because we need to work on a few things. However, we're not going to talk about what's been going wrong. Instead, let's talk about the times when things have been working a little better and how we want things to be."

OR

"This is what I see that is working for (student name). What do you see that is working?"

PURPOSE

(e.g., problem definition, goals, desires, need)

To the student: What reason do you think we have for meeting today? What reason will your parents or I give?

_____

_____

_____

To parents and yourself: What do you hope happens in our time today?

_____

_____

_____

I hope . . .

_____

_____

_____

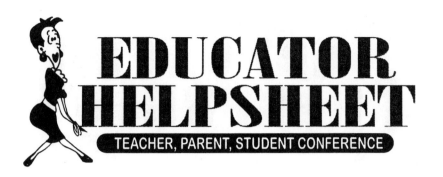

MASTER 59 Continued

If a problem is shared, make sure you externalize it from the child; normalize and emphasize that it does not occur 100% of the time. When others share problems, make sure they feel heard and understood.

Reflect _____ Externalize _____ Labelize _____

Normalize _____ Temporize _____

POTENTIAL

(solutions, exceptions; get as many and as much detail as you can)

To all: In what class(es) or (where) are things better? Describe how that is accomplished. When in the past have things worked? What is working now?

_____

_____

_____

I have seen (student) do this. Describe how, when, where. Share examples.

_____

_____

_____

For the student: How did you accomplish these times? What do teachers/parents/others do that helps this happen? Continue asking:

When else does this or has this occurred?

_____

_____

_____

(continued)

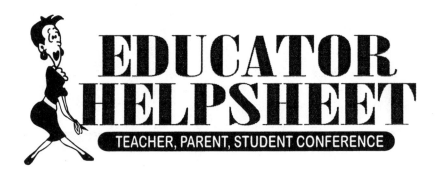

MASTER 59 Continued

To all present: How do you want things to be? How will all of us know when things are better? (The student may think things are OK now; if that is the case, do a little more work on the problem or share an idea and ask the student whether that sounds better.) What will we see happening that will tell us things are better? (remember—everyone involved answers)

_____

_____

Potentials:

PLAN:

For all: For the next week (days), if we were to do more of what we have all said works slightly better, what would we see each other doing more of?

Personal _____ Positive _____ Process _____

Precise _____ Present _____

If necessary, discuss **potential** roadblocks to make a **plan** of counterattack. Set up a time frame for follow-up. Restate the **plan.**

_____

_____

Summarize with a solution statement (restate **potentials**) and the assumption that the **plan** (solution) will begin happening immediately. Copies for all involved finalizes the feeling of an equal partnership. Handshakes among all, especially with the student, are a nice ending.

_____

_____

Willyn H. Webb, *The Educator's Guide to Solutioning.* Copyright © 1999 by Corwin Press, Inc.

MASTER 60

Let's Celebrate Progress

Dear _____:

Just wanted to follow up on our conference. Your responses to the questions will help us monitor **progress** and find out what is working!

What did you think was valuable during our time together?

_____

_____

Which parts of the **plan** have been the most successful?

_____

_____

How did you, the student, and I do that? Describe details of different, better behaviors; skills; and so on.

_____

_____

How can we use what has been exceptional to solve any other concerns?

_____

_____

How can we continue the **progress** that has been made?

_____

_____

Any other comments?

_____

_____

Let's keep this process going. It's working!

Spread Your Wings Once the language of solutioning is an integral element of your personal script, you will be amazed at when and where and how effectively it comes out.

The Last Day Debate

A teacher's meeting at the end of the year was full of heated discussion regarding how the last day of school was to be spent. The teachers in the room were hot, tired, and frustrated with middle school students experiencing spring fever. The debate became more heated, with teachers teaming up against each other either for a play day or a test day. Feeling solutioning focused, I simply asked, "What has worked the best before?" Everyone got quiet for a moment and began thinking about something that had worked instead of continuing to complain about students and how they needed to be controlled or how we couldn't get good testing conditions, and so on. The silence was a nice breather, if nothing else. Then a master teacher, who was very respected by the staff, picked up on my question and shared her version of the best last day of school during her 23-year teaching career. Some others nodded that they had also liked that year. Another teacher shared a similar procedure at her old school, and the discussion turned into a vision of what works and what could be, instead of a debate and a battle.

Solutioned Staffing

From Kathy Lemon, fifth- and sixth-grade counselor (Used with permission from Kathy Lemon)

Kathy shared that while taking my course on solutioning, she found herself in a tense special education staffing. The student was not having much success, and the recommendation was for more special education that the student and the parents were against. The special education staff was making a very good case for why the student needed more hours in the program, which was very depressing to hear. Finally, Kathy asked, "What can Joe do well?" which led to a completely different, and much needed, discussion. Amazingly, there were skills and abilities. When the mood was better, she asked Joe, "How do you want things to be?" He answered that he thought he only needed 2 hours per day of special education. She followed with, "What can you do differently to make it that way?" Joe proceeded to give a full discourse on study habits, good behavior, and persistent effort, which he was willing to try to keep from having more special education. Kathy said it was such a nice change because Joe was motivating to listen to. The **plan** that resulted in the staffing was a trial period during which Joe would use his **plan** to stay out of more special education. Kathy summed it up for them: "When Joe is using good study habits, good behavior, and persistent effort in his classes and does not require more special education, let's meet again and talk about everything he does that works. Is 2 weeks long enough?" (assumed success)

By spreading your wings just a little, you can start the ripple effect. If you are in a position of leading meetings from staffings, to accountability groups, to school boards, you will be able to use the 3-P process itself in organizing the flow of the meeting. MASTER 61 "Educator Helpsheet: Meeting Solution Style" will assist you in setting a solutioned agenda.

MASTER 61

Purpose: Everyone likes to know why he or she is at a meeting. The meeting may have more than one **purpose**, but they can all be summarized at the beginning. Then take the first **purpose** and proceed through the solutioning process.

What are the **purposes** of the meeting? Prioritize the order.

_____

_____

_____

_____

Potentials: Share what is working that will lead to fulfillment of the **purpose.** Use the questions of solutioning to focus on exceptions and **potentials** for involving the participants. This will limit input to effective, usable information and limit whining, complaining, and blaming. You may want to have a few appropriate questions preselected for each step.

Which questions will best facilitate our discussion for each **purpose?**

_____

_____

_____

_____

_____

_____

Willyn H. Webb, *The Educator's Guide to Solutioning.* Copyright © 1999 by Corwin Press, Inc.

MASTER 61 Continued

Plan: End each discussion with an agreed-on **plan** that meets the Fab Five criteria. Use questions to form it, and everyone will feel invested it in. Set up time frames for **progress** and move on to the next **purpose.**

What **plan** questions could I ask?

_____

_____

_____

_____

Progress: Some items may be updates. If this is the case, use the questions for **progress** to help focus on what was effective, successful, and valuable. Project **progress** into the future by giving responsibility and by looking at how it was accomplished.

_____

_____

_____

_____

_____

_____

_____

Using solutioning in meetings, staffings, workroom discussions, and on and on will give you a sense of power and make your positive influence more productive. You can turn the tide, whether you are running the entire meeting or are a single participant. Shift the focus of the situation from the past to the future, from blaming to choosing, from problems to solutions. Not only will you benefit, but so will all of those with whom you interact—most of all the students. **A Positive Agenda**

A teacher affects eternity; no one can tell where his/her influence stops. (Henry Adams in Peter, 1977, p. 464)

Solutioning walks the walk through our most valuable educational resources—ourselves and the words we use to interact with students. **Chapter 7 Focused**

Much is written on the "touchy feely" side of teaching. Many new positive gurus and motivational speakers talk a talk similar to the solutioning focus. However, *creating* solutioning-focused interactions, learning, and learners is the part many leave out. Solutioning strives to walk the walk through our most valuable educational resources—ourselves and the words we use to interact with students. Use yourself, train yourself, and speak solutioning. No new curriculum or programs, just you and a few questions empower the focus. The result is responsible, positive learners who *practice* self-control, take responsibility, and experience success.

Take a second and glance back at some of the comparison charts throughout this book. Look only at the problem-focused, traditional side. Is this the way you want to spend your day—controlling? Battling? Blaming? Trying to fix problems? How about your students?

Now look at the solutioning side—partnering, forward moving, asking, positive, empowered. Feel better? Is this a way you could *now* spend your day? How would your students respond? Which solutioning questions/ideas are you going to try first?

Mankind owes to the child the best it has to give. (U.N. Declaration)

Training Resources

The following role-play scripts will facilitate your practice with the language of solutioning. Grab a partner to read the student's lines, and you will be able to get a feel for the 3-P process. A scenario is provided for each level (elementary, middle level, and high school), but practicing with all three is recommended. Have fun!

The Boxing Match: Elementary

Educator: Tom, did you just hit Andy?

Tom: He took my scissors. He's a jerk.

Educator: Tom, what would be different if you controlled your anger and didn't hit other students? (externalize problem—question for positive consequences)

Tom: What would happen if I never hit? He'd take my scissors.

Educator: Yeah, he might, but are there enough scissors for everyone? Which works better—getting other scissors or hitting and getting in trouble? (reflect, question consequences)

Tom: I hate getting in trouble, but he's a jerk.

Educator: Have you ever kept your own scissors, or pencil, or anything anywhere and not gotten so mad you hit? (reflect—exception question)

Tom: At home, I get slapped if I hit my sister when she takes my stuff, so I watch it there. If Mom's around, I tell my sister I'll get her later and she stops.

Educator: So, you can control anger when you don't want to be slapped. (solution statement, highlight exception) Would being friends with Andy or not getting in trouble with me be reasons to control anger?

Tom: That would be kinda cool, but I don't like it when someone takes my stuff.

Educator: No one likes that. (normalize problem) Now that we know you can control anger, what could you do instead of hitting and still keep your scissors? (**plan** question)

Tom: (shrug)

Educator: Can you pretend yourself doing something different? (*pretend potential* question)

Tom: No.

Educator: OK, what do the other students do? Could you borrow any ideas from them? (*people potential* question)

Tom: I saw Jeff try to take Andy's scissors one time, and Andy just told him to get his own and he did.

Educator: That's an idea.

Tom: I could probably do that, but I don't know if it would work.

Educator: Pretend someone is trying to take something of yours and you tell that person to get his or her own. What are you doing? (pretend **plan**—solution rehearsal)

Tom: I am mad, but I keep it in and stop before I hit. I say, "Get your own" like I mean it.

Educator: Sounds like a **plan** to me. Ready to give it a try?

Tom: OK.

Educator: How long do you think you will need to do it before you can tell me about how well it works? A day?

Tom: Yeah.

Educator: OK, let's talk tomorrow morning 'cause I'll like hearing about how you control anger and tell them to get their own. (restate **plan**—assume success)

Putting It All Together: Middle Level

Educator: Chantal, you are missing five assignments and your grade right now is a D. Grades come out next week, and you are very close to failing.

Chantal: Well, I hate this class. It is so boring. (angry, problem statement)

Educator: (curious tone) So, failing is OK with you because of boredom? (questioning for consequences, externalizing)

Chantal: No, I want to pass. I'd just die if I had to repeat a class, and my parents would kill me.

Educator: You want to pass, so our **purpose** here is to find out how that can happen despite boredom. (externalize, joint **purpose**)

Chantal: Yeah, I guess I want to pass with at least a C. (**purpose** statement)

Educator: When in the past have you been able to control boredom and pass? (question for *past potential*— problem exception)

Chantal: Well, last year I hated math. It is just a bunch of numbers, but then I started thinking about it as money or real-life stuff, and I could get into it. (exception—**potential** solution)

Educator: Cool, so when you thought of it in real-life ways, you were able to overcome boredom and do it. (solution statement, restate **potential**) Do you still do some of that now, thinking of school in real-life ways? (question for *present potential*, tie past into present)

Chantal: Yeah, I guess I still do it in math, and now that I think about it, last week we were learning the metric system in science. I thought about some of it like track or cooking and stuff. I kind of told myself it was more real than school so I would pass. (*present potential*)

Educator: It sounds to me as if you are really good at beating boredom and passing your other classes. (solution statement) How might using real-life ideas work here in English? (move toward a **plan**)

Chantal: English could be real life too, I guess. I like some magazines, and they have writing in them. (thinking—pause) I write notes to my friends a lot, and they hate it when they can't figure out a word I've spelled wrong. I write Christmas lists, and I used to have a diary. That's not boring. (*present potential* solution)

Educator: Sounds as if you already have some real-life ways to think about English and beat boredom. Do you think you could try what has worked so well for you in math—the thinking real life—this week in English? (solution statement, **plan** question)

Chantal: I don't know. It might work. It does in math. I don't want boredom to make me flunk. I'll try real-life stuff for English and see if it helps. (**plan**)

Educator: Sounds like a **plan**. Let's talk again 1 week from today, and you can tell me about your real-life thinking and we can celebrate victory over boredom and a C, OK? (time frame, assumed success)

Chantal: OK.

Last Ditch: High School

Melissa was a sophomore who lived with a single father who I suspected had a drinking problem. He had come to register Melissa, smelling of alcohol. Melissa had an after-school job at a fast-food restaurant. She was a decent student and had some positive friends but also seemed to connect with a crowd of students who often missed and had been in trouble for drugs. Melissa seemed to be one of those students who could go either way. The more aggressive/authoritarian adults were, the more she would retaliate with anger and yelling—getting them nowhere. A few questions allow Melissa to take responsibility and analyze her choices, rather than get angry with another adult and shut out another positive influence. The entire dialogue takes only a few minutes but makes a real difference.

Educator:　Melissa, could I have your excuse for yesterday?

Melissa:　No. (defensively)

Educator:　You sound a little upset, and I know you are aware that excuses are required. Is there something we could talk about?

Melissa:　Look, I've had a lot going on lately, and school just wasn't gonna happen yesterday. I needed to chill for a while. So just get off my case about the excuse already.

Educator:　So, chilling out worked for you enough that you were able to come to school today. (**potential** solution statement)

Melissa:　(softening a little) I guess, but I don't feel that great about yesterday.

Educator:　What works better for you—coming to school or ditching? (**purpose** question)

Melissa:　Coming is easier, then I don't have teachers on my butt for an excuse or makeup work. Yesterday just sucked.

Educator:　So, when things suck and you still come to school, what is different? (assume problem exception, ask for *past potential*)

Melissa:　I don't know. Either I don't find anybody to ditch with, or we don't have any money for it. By lunch, I usually get in the groove, and my girls help me a lot.

Educator:　So, coming to school and talking with your friends sounds as if it helps more than ditching, plus there aren't the hassles of excuses and makeup. (solution statement)

Melissa:　It just ain't worth it, you know. I'm not gonna ditch anymore. It makes things worse.

Educator:　How are you going to do that—not ditch? (question to form **plan** in positive)

Melissa:　When I'm having a bum day, I'll just talk to my girls instead of looking for a way out. I'll avoid the dudes I ditch with, and leave my money at home.

Educator:　That sounds like a **plan**. Let's talk again in a week when coming and talking to the girls is helping on bum days. You can tell me about how good it works. There's also a school counselor who is cool, if you ever need to talk more. Now let's get to work. I'll write you an unexcused absence note, and you'll still lose the points, but it's the last time, so it shouldn't affect your grade too much. (restate *positive plan,* assume success, maintain consequences)

Melissa:　Cool.

References

Allen, H. (1998). Changed by a challenge. *Decision, 39*(3), 4-5.

Ames, C. (1992). Classrooms: Goals, structures, and student motivation. *Journal of Educational Psychology, 84*(3), 261-271.

Andrews, J., & Andrews, M. (1995). Solution-focused assumptions that support family-centered early interventions. *Infants and Young Children, 8*(1), 60-67.

Bonnington, S. B. (1993). Solution-focused brief therapy: Helpful interventions for school counselors. *The School Counselor, 41*(2), 126-127.

Brewer, E. W., Dunn, J. O., & Olszewski, P. (1988). Extrinsic reward and intrinsic motivation: The vital link between classroom management and student performance. *Journal of Education for Teaching, 14*(2), 151-170.

Budman, S., & Gurman, A. (1988). *Theory and practice of brief therapy.* New York: Guilford.

Campbell, L. P. (1995). P.A.C.E.: A student problem-solving process that works. *Education, 116*(2), 272-273.

Carpenter, J. (1997). Editorial: Investigating brief solution-focused therapy. *Journal of Family Therapy, 19*(2), 117-120.

Czyzewski, K. M. (1996). Rapid EAP: Solution-focused therapy in employee assistance. *EAP Digest, 16*(2), 16-19.

Davis, A. M. (1986). Dispute resolution at an early age. *Negotiation Journal, 3*(7), 287-297.

Deci, E. L., & Flaste, R. (1995). *Why we do what we do: The dynamics of personal autonomy.* New York: G. P. Putnam.

Denby, J. (1995). Elementary kids in parent-teacher conferences. *Education Digest, 61*(3), 45-47.

de Shazer, S. (1985). *Keys to solutions in brief therapy.* New York: Norton.

de Shazer, S. (1988). *Clues: Investigating solutions in brief therapy.* New York: Norton.

de Shazer, S., Berg, I. K., Lipchik, E., Nunnally, E., Molnar, A., Gingerich, W., & Weiner-Davis, M. (1986). Brief therapy: Focused solution development. *Family Process, 25*(2), 207-222.

Dolan, Y. M. (1991). *Resolving sexual abuse: Solution-focused therapy and Ericksonian hypnosis.* New York: Norton.

Downing, J., & Harrison, T. (1992). Solutions and school counseling. *The School Counselor, 39*(5), 327-331.

Eaton, M., & Pougiales, R. (1993). Work, reflection, and community: Conditions that support writing self-evaluations. *New Directions for Teaching and Learning, 56,* 47-63.

Elam, S., et al. (1994). The 26th annual Phi Delta Kappa/Gallup poll of the public's attitudes toward the public schools. *Phi Delta Kappan, 76*(1), 41-56.

Elam, S., & Rose, L. C. (1995). The 27th annual Phi Delta Kappa/Gallup poll of the public's attitudes toward the public schools. *Phi Delta Kappan, 77*(1), 41-56.

Enoch, S. W. (1995). Better parent-teacher conferences. *School Administrator, 52,* 24-26.

Epstein, G. (1990). The power of imagery. *New Realities, 10*(3), 11, 52-53.

Friedman, S., & Fanger, M. T. (1991). *Expanding therapeutic possibilities.* Lexington, MA: Lexington.

Furman, B., & Ahola, T. (1992). *Solution talk: Hosting therapeutic conversations.* New York: Norton.

Furtwengler, W. J. (1996). Improving secondary school discipline by involving students in the process. *NAASP Bulletin, 80*(581), 36-43.

Gass, M., & Gillis, H. L. (1995). Focusing on the "solution" rather than the "problem": Empowering client change in adventure experiences. *Journal of Experiential Education, 18*(2), 63-69.

Goldberg, A. (1995). Mental rehearsal for peak performance. *Swimming Technique, 31*(4), 24-26.

Gootman, M. E. (1997). *The caring teacher's guide to discipline: Helping young students learn self-control, responsibility, and respect.* Thousand Oaks, CA: Corwin.

Hancock, A. (1994). Violence: Missouri schools focus on prevention. *School and Community, 80*(3), 8-11.

Heller, G. S. (1996). Changing the school to reduce student violence: What works? *NASSP Bulletin, 80*(579), 1-9.

Huber, C. H., & Backlund, B. A. (1996). *The 20-minute counselor.* New York: Crossroad.

Hunter, M. (1967). *Motivation theory from teachers.* El Segundo, CA: TIP.

Hwang, Y. G. (1995). Student apathy, lack of self-responsibility, and false self-esteem are failing American schools. *Education, 115*(4), 484-489.

Johnson, D. W., & Johnson, R. T. (1996). Reducing school violence through conflict resolution training. *NASSP Bulletin, 80*(579), 11-17.

Juhnke, G., & Coker, J. K. (1997). A solution-focused intervention with recovering, alcohol-dependent, single-parent mothers and their children. *Journal of Addictions and Offender Counseling, 17,* 77-87.

Juhnke, G., & Osborne, L. (1997). The solution-focused debriefing group: An integrated postviolence group intervention for adults. *Journal for Specialists in Group Work, 22*(1), 66-76.

Killin, T. E., & Williams, R. L. (1995). Making a difference in school climate, counseling services, and student success. *NASSP Bulletin, 79*(570), 44-51.

Klar, H., & Coleman, W. L. (1995). Brief solution-focused strategies for behavioral pediatrics. *Family-Focused Pediatrics, 42,* 131-141.

Klein, J. D., & Pridemore, D. R. (1994). Effects of orienting activities and practice on achievement, continuing motivation, and student behaviors in a cooperative learning environment. *Educational Technology Research & Development, 42*(4), 41-54.

Kohn, A. (1995). Discipline is the problem—not the solution. *Learning, 24*(3), 34.

Kral, R., & Kowalski, K. (1989). After the miracle: The second stage in solution-focused brief therapy. *Journal of Strategic and Systemic Therapies, 8*(2-3), 73-76.

Lepper, M. R., & Hodell, M. (1989). Intrinsic motivation in the classroom. In C. Ames & R. Ames (Eds.), *Research on motivation in education* (Vol. 3, pp. 73-105). San Diego: Academic Press.

Lincoln, W. (1993). Helping students develop self-discipline. *Learning, 22*(3), 38-41.

Malone, T. W., & Lepper, M. R. (1987). Making learning fun: A taxonomy of intrinsic motivation for learning. In R. E. Snow & M. J. Farr (Eds.), *Aptitude, learning, and instruction* (Vol. 3). Mahwah, NJ: Lawrence Erlbaum.

Mason, W. H., Breen, R. Y., & Whipple, W. R. (1994). Solution-focused therapy and inpatient psychiatric nursing. *Journal of Psychosocial Nursing, 32*(10), 46-49.

Mendler, A. N. (1992). *What do I do when . . .?* Bloomington, IN: National Educational Service.

Metcalf, L. (1995). *Counseling toward solutions: A practical solution-focused program for working with students, teachers, and parents.* New York: Center for Applied Research in Education.

Metcalf, L. (1997). *Parenting toward solutions: How parents can use skills they already have to raise responsible, loving kids.* Englewood Cliffs, NJ: Prentice Hall.

Molnar, A., & de Shazer, S. (1987). Solution-focused therapy: Toward the identification of therapeutic tasks. *Journal of Marital and Family Therapy, 13*(4), 349-358.

Morganett, L. L. (1991). Good teacher-student relationships: A key element in classroom motivation and management. *Education, 112*(2), 260-264.

Morganett, L. L. (1996). Activities for improving student motivation and classroom climate. *Kappa Delta Pi Record, 32*(4), 148-150.

Moyers, S. (1994). Making elementary-schoolers a part of parent conferences. *Education Digest, 60*(4), 57-60.

Murphy, J. J. (1994). Working with what works: A solution-focused approach to school behavior problems. *The School Counselor, 42*(1), 59-65.

O'Hanlon, B., & Beadle, S. (1994). *A field guide to possibility land: Possibility therapy methods.* Omaha, NE: Possibility Press.

O'Hanlon, W. (1996). *The handout book.* Omaha, NE: Possibility Press.

O'Hanlon, W., & Weiner-Davis, M. (1989). *In search of solutions: A new direction in psychotherapy.* New York: Norton.

Peter, L. J. (1977). *Peter's quotations: Ideas for our time.* New York: William Morrow.

Rhodes, J. (1993). The use of solution-focused brief therapy in schools. *Educational Psychology in Practice, 9*(1), 27-34.

Rose, L. C., Gallup, A. M., & Elam, S. M. (1997). The 29th annual Phi Delta Kappa/Gallup poll of the public's attitudes toward the public schools. *Phi Delta Kappan, 79*(1), 41-56.

Schlessinger, L. (1994). *Ten stupid things women do to mess up their lives.* New York: HarperCollins.

Short, R. J., & Short, P. M. (1992). An organizational perspective on student discipline. *Education, 114*(4), 567-569.

Simmons, B. J. (1991). Parent-teacher conferences: Making them more productive. *Kappa Delta Pi Record, 27*(4), 120-122.

Smith, D. D., & Riveria, D. P. (1995). Discipline in special education and general education settings. *Focus on Exceptional Children, 27*(5), 1-14.

Sparks, W. G. (1993). Promoting self-responsibility and decision making with at-risk students. *Journal of Physical Education, Recreation, and Dance, 64*(2), 74-79.

Stewart, S. (1996). The blame game: Why can't we accept responsibility? *Youth, 16*(2), 3-4.

Tierno, M. J. (1998). Building a positive classroom environment. In T. Rusnak (Ed.), *An integrated approach to character education* (pp. 57-68). Thousand Oaks, CA: Corwin.

Tuyn, L. K. (1992). Solution-oriented therapy and Rogerian nursing science: An integrated approach. *Archives of Psychiatric Nursing, 6*(2), 83-89.

Vannoy, S. (1994). *The ten greatest gifts I give my children.* New York: Fireside.

Walter, J. L., & Peller, J. E. (1992). *Becoming solution-focused in brief therapy.* New York: Bruner-Mazel.

Washburn, P. (1994). Advantages of brief solution-oriented focus in home-based family preservation services. *Journal of Systemic Therapies, 13*(2), 47-57.

Weakland, J. H., Fisch, R., Watzlawick, P., & Bodin, A. M. (1974). Brief therapy: Focused problem resolution. *Family Process, 13*(2), 141-168.

Webb, W. (1999). *Solutioning: Solution-focused interventions for counselors.* Philadelphia: Taylor and Francis/Accelerated Development.

Webster's 21st century book of quotations. (1992). Nashville, TN: Thomas Nelson.

White, M., & Epston, D. (1990). *Narrative means to therapeutic ends.* New York: Norton.

Zimmerman, J., & Coyle, V. (1991, March/April). Council: Reviving the art of listening. *Utne Reader,* 79-85.

Index

CORWIN
PRESS

The Corwin Press logo—a raven striding across an open book—represents the happy union of courage and learning. We are a professional-level publisher of books and journals for K–12 educators, and we are committed to creating and providing resources that embody these qualities. Corwin's motto is "Success for All Learners."